Read all of the Puffin nonfiction books!

Our Choice: How We Can
Solve the Climate Crisis
Al Gore

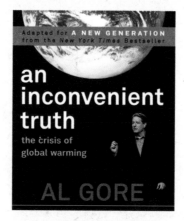

An Inconvenient Truth:
The Crisis of Global Warming
Al Gore

Three Cups of Tea:
One Man's Journey to Change the
World . . . One Child at a Time
Greg Mortenson & David Oliver Relin

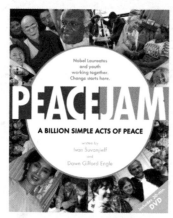

PeaceJam:
A Billion Simple Acts of Peace
Ivan Suvanjieff and
Dawn Gifford Engle

Animals and Habitats of
the United States
Jeff Corwin

GIRLS GONE GREEN

LYNN HIRSHFIELD

participant° MEDIA

PUFFIN BOOKS
An Imprint of Penguin Group (USA) Inc.

PUFFIN BOOKS

Published by the Penguin Group
Penguin Young Readers Group,
345 Hudson Street, New York, New York 10014, U.S.A.
Penguin Group (USA) Inc., 375 Hudson Street, New York, New York 10014, U.S.A.
Penguin Group (Canada), 90 Eglinton Avenue East, Suite 700,
Toronto, Ontario, Canada M4P 2Y3 (a division of Pearson Penguin Canada Inc.)
Penguin Books Ltd, 80 Strand, London WC2R 0RL, England
Penguin Ireland, 25 St Stephen's Green, Dublin 2, Ireland (a division of Penguin Books Ltd)
Penguin Group (Australia), 250 Camberwell Road, Camberwell,
Victoria 3124, Australia (a division of Pearson Australia Group Pty Ltd)
Penguin Books India Pvt Ltd, 11 Community Centre,
Panchsheel Park, New Delhi – 110 017, India
Penguin Group (NZ), 67 Apollo Drive, Rosedale, North Shore 0632, New Zealand
(a division of Pearson New Zealand Ltd.)
Penguin Books (South Africa) (Pty) Ltd, 24 Sturdee Avenue,
Rosebank, Johannesburg 2196, South Africa

Registered Offices: Penguin Books Ltd, 80 Strand, London WC2R 0RL, England

10 9 8 7 6 5 4 3 2 1

LIBRARY OF CONGRESS CATALOGING-IN-PUBLICATION DATA
Hirshfield, Lynn.
Girls gone green / Lynn Hirshfield.
p. cm.
ISBN 978-0-14-241406-4
1. Environmentalism—Juvenile literature. 2. Environmental protection—Citizen participation—
Juvenile literature. 3. Green movement—Juvenile literature. 4. Girls—Juvenile literature. I. Title.
GE195.5.H57 2010   333.72—dc22   2009011394

Printed in the United States of America

Book design by Tony Sahara
Illustrations © 2010 by Tony Sahara

Some of the text is set in Nanonymus Eco Sans, also known as Ecofont,
which was created by SPRANQ creative communications based
in Utrecht, The Netherlands.
By omitting parts of each letter, your ink cartridges (or toner) last longer,
since up to 20 percent less ink is used to create each letter.

www.ecofont.eu/ecofont_en.html

ECO-FRIENDLY BOOKS
Made in the USA

THIS BOOK IS DEDICATED TO
LARISSA PELTOLA FOR HELPING ME KEEP IT REAL.
THANK YOU FOR BEING MY PERSONAL GREEN GIRL
GUINEA PIG DURING YOUR AFTER-SCHOOL VISITS
TO MY OFFICE. I CAN REST EASY KNOWING THAT
THE FUTURE OF OUR PLANET IS IN THE
HANDS OF PASSIONATE YOUNG
ACTIVISTS LIKE YOU.
LOVE,
AUNTIE LYNN

Table of Contents

Foreword by **Hayden Panettiere**
for **SAVE THE WHALES AGAIN!**

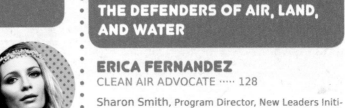

Foreword by Hayden Panettiere

For actress and activist Hayden Panettiere, being green means looking below the surface.

Anyone who knows me knows how much I love animals and how passionate I am about protecting them. So when Jeff Pantukhoff, president and founder of the Whaleman Foundation, approached me about being their spokesperson five years ago, I jumped at the opportunity!

The Whaleman Foundation is a nonprofit organization whose primary mission is to raise public awareness of the issues that affect cetaceans (dolphins, whales, and porpoises) and their ocean habitats through their research, films, and public outreach campaigns. When I heard about the plight of the whales and the work the Whaleman Foundation was doing, getting involved was a no-brainer for me.

I've learned so much since becoming a part of the foundation's efforts. Soon after I agreed to help, Jeff took my mother, Lesley, and me on our very first trip to San Ignacio Lagoon in Baja Mexico, the only undeveloped mating and birthing ground for the California gray whale. It was a truly amazing experience. Along with seeing all of the beautiful gray whales and their newborns firsthand, I also learned about the threats that they face along with other whales and dolphins, such as loss of habitat, entanglement in fishing nets, toxic and noise pollution, global warming, increasing and expanding whaling—the list

SAVE THE WHALES AGAIN!
www.savethewhalesagain.org

SAVE THE WHALES AGAIN!

goes on and on. It was on this trip that Jeff showed me a short film and explained to me his vision and goals for the Save the Whales Again! campaign.

The goals of our campaign are to end whaling worldwide while raising awareness to the other threats whales and dolphins face. There is a brutal practice in Japan that has unnecessarily and painfully taken the lives of hundreds of thousands of dolphins and other small whales. They blind and frighten these helpless animals by hammering on metal poles in the water, driving them into small coves where they are trapped in nets and then killed. I experienced this firsthand on a trip with our team to Taiji, Japan, in 2007. There we paddled out into the bloodred waters of the killing cove, where over thirty pilot whales had already been slaughtered. With fellow activists, I honored the beautiful animals that had lost their lives there while unveiling the truth to the world. During our peaceful ceremony, the Japanese fisherman, unprovoked, became violent and physically aggressive toward us. After being hit with large poles and threatened with spinning boat propellers, which came inches from us, we held our ground. The media attention generated by the incident was massive, and it became one of the largest steps toward victory since the whaling moratorium was put in place in 1986. I am aware this fight will not end overnight, but I am committed to seeing this battle through until the very end.

My tip to you is to take action on a cause that is important to you. Use the stories of the green girls in this book as your inspiration. They are taking action on so many different causes and making amazing progress on behalf of our planet. And so can you! You can help me protect the whales and dolphins that call our oceans their home. With your help, these beautiful and intelligent creatures will be saved.

For more information, please visit www.savethewhalesagain.org and learn how you can get involved.

—Hayden

CHAPTER 1

THE BEAUTY ENTREPRENEURS AND FASHIONISTAS

Green Teen Beauty

Erin Schrode

Age: 17
Hometown:
Marin County,
California

MEET ERIN AND HER CAUSE

I'm Erin Schrode. I live in Marin County, California, and I'm seventeen years old. I fill my days with friends, family, and things that are fun and unique to being me. I am always eager to go out and spread the green word—doing things like blogging, hosting events, writing, and acting as a spokesperson for the Teens Turning Green campaign (more to come on that!). I like to think that I am a "young eco-renaissance woman"—sounds fancy, right?!

I became an activist watching my mother take action on issues. When I was ten, my mother found out there was a higher-than-normal incidence of cancer in our community. She not only committed herself to searching for a cause, she started a movement. She pulled together volunteers and raised awareness of the problem. I went with her to talk to our neighbors and witnessed how people reacted when they were told about the issue. They were shocked and grateful for my mom's efforts, and wanted to know more. I was proud of my mom's work. She inspired me to speak out and act on causes that I connected with, and a few years later, I found an important one to stand behind.

When I was thirteen years old, I started wearing make-up, like all my friends. I decided one day to read the labels and discovered that there were harmful toxins in many of my products. I took my research a step further, read the labels on my shampoo, toothpaste, and deodorant, and did some Web searches for these chemicals. I was horrified by what I saw. Eighty-nine percent of the more than six thousand chemicals in these products have never been tested for human safety. In fact, these beauty products are not even regulated by government agencies! Chemicals like parabens, sodium lauryl sulfate, coal tars, and other incomprehensible words (butylated hydroxy-toluene, anyone?!) appear frequently on the labels of these types of products. Propylene glycol is a key ingredient in antifreeze; petrolatum is addictive; and formaldehyde pre-serves dead bodies—and I was putting this on my skin! In doing some more digging, I found that the problem with using these chemicals on our bodies is that whatever goes onto our skin enters our bloodstream. Once they are in our bloodstream, they can cause cancer, contaminate our organ systems, and give us allergies, among other terrible things. After I read all these facts, I knew I wanted to keep chemicals out of my body. But by no means was I going to say no to makeup, shampoo, deodorant, or toothpaste! I treasure my ruby-red nails, hate B.O., crave silky hair, love white teeth, and live for a clean face. There had to be an alternative.

TEENS UNITE TO FOUND TEENS FOR SAFE COSMETICS

I went to my mom and some of my friends and shared my concerns. After I told them about all the harmful chemicals that we are exposed to every day, they felt the same way I did! We all heard the call to action and were impassioned to do something to get the word out and try to make a change. And where better to initiate change than with our own bodies? So together we started Teens for Safe Cosmetics (TSC), now known as

Teens Turning Green. Our organization strives to inform young people about how to live a green life, beginning with safer and healthier choices in cosmetics and personal-care prod-ucts. Our goal is to make changes in a positive way through legislation and partnerships with companies that are already doing right by our bodies and planet. And we hope to urge change in the beauty industry and the world

beyond. We knew that if we as teens united as one voice, we could make ourselves heard.

It wasn't easy getting Teens for Safe Cosmetics off the ground and establishing a presence. We faced some serious opposition from the powerful beauty industry lobby. TSC fights for the passage of laws that will require companies that sell cosmetics and personal-care products to disclose ingredients, remove certain chemicals, and take responsibility for their actions. But the beauty industry has continued to put up road-blocks on efforts we make to have our voices heard. It's also been a challenge to get our message out to the public. For example, teen magazines advertise only commercial beauty brands, so it has been difficult for them to put us on their pages without angering their sponsors. But fortunately that is starting to change. *O Magazine* and *Vogue* recently covered the issue of greening the beauty industry, and I look forward to *Teen Vogue* and *Seventeen* following suit. Overall, the green beauty movement is getting huge and making big strides in educating consumers about healthy and safe products. And TSC

Judi Shils

Executive Director, Teens Turning Green

Judi Shils is Erin Schrode's mother and mentor, and she helped Erin launch Teens for Safe Cosmetics. Judi formed the Marin Cancer Project (now called Search for a Cause) after community members expressed concerns about high cancer rates in their neighborhoods.

If you want to follow Erin's and Judi's lead and take a stand in your community, you can visit the Teens Turning Green Web site and learn about starting a chapter in your town. Go to www.teensturninggreen.org for more information.

Judi's Tip

Did you know that in 2007, the Campaign for Safe Cosmetics found lead in leading brands of lipstick? Two-thirds of the thirty-three samples tested contained detectable levels of lead. Lead exposure can lead to many health problems, including seizures, brain damage, anemia, and kidney damage. Make sure you know what's in your lipstick. Be aware, ask questions at your cosmetics counter, and do your research. Great lead-free brands include Iredale Mineral Cosmetics, Dr. Hauschka, Hemp Organics, Burt's Bees, Lavera & Lavere, and Logona.

has been doing its part to help with this, but our work is just beginning. Although most of our members are not old enough to vote, we can still have a voice in our government—a strong, truthful, raw voice with a fresh perspective to which politicians, lobbyists, and media will have to listen.

A CHANCE TO HAVE OUR VOICES HEARD

In 2005, TSC members went to Sacramento, California, to speak with Governor Arnold Schwarzenegger's staff on the importance of the Safe Cosmetics Act of 2005 (SB 484), a bill that requires cosmetics manufacturers to disclose to consumers ingredients known to cause cancer and birth defects, and permits the state to access all health-related ingredient

Amy Galper
Founder, Buddha Nose

One of Erin's mentors is Amy Galper, a groovy grown-up green girl who is helping develop a lip balm for the Teens Turning Green collection.

Amy Galper believes that finding a moment of stillness may be all that's needed to awaken our eco-consciousness. Several years ago, Amy was diagnosed with a rare kidney disease. She changed her lifestyle, and began following a macrobiotic diet and doing acupuncture and bodywork. With this new life change, she was inspired to develop an organic line of body-care products, known as Buddha Nose.

Amy's Tip

If you don't have access to green cosmetics in your neighborhood, here are a few natural recipes for beauty products you can make at home:

HONEY MASK: Cover your entire face with a thin layer of organic honey, let sit for ten minutes, and rinse with warm water. This is great for balancing skin to help prevent breakouts.

SUGAR SCRUB: Mix together 1 cup of organic sugar, 2 to 4 tablespoons of olive oil, 1 teaspoon of lemon juice, and a drop of your favorite essential oil. Use over your entire body for exfoliation and skin balancing. Rinse with warm water.

There are many fabulous ways to go green.

Here are a few green alternatives that you can throw in your makeup bag:

- Nude Lip Balm
- Dr. Hauschka Mascara
- Astara Mask
- EO Hand Sanitizer
- Priti Nail Polish

information. We met with his legislative aide and spoke passionately about our concerns and the need for the governor's support for the bill. He was extremely encouraging and commended us for taking action.

Soon after TSC's visit to Sacramento, the bill was passed. This was a true landmark, and TSC did its part! The issue of chemical policy is relevant to all aspects of life: lead in paint, pesticides on crops, flame retardants on furniture and clothing, volatile organic compounds (VOCs) in carpets and paints, etc. I have personally followed up by testifying on the issue and have traveled to the California state capitol to lobby for two bills regarding the removal of lead from lipsticks and bisphenol A (BPA) from baby bottles. Other TSC members and I had the opportunity to meet with politicians and tell our personal stories. As teenagers, to look into the eyes of politicians and know that our words have a direct impact on the government is an extraordinary experience!

DOING THINGS LOCALLY WITH TTG

Teens for Safe Cosmetics has grown and evolved into Teens Turning Green (TTG). Some of the fun things I am involved in are organizing fashion shows, green spas, and public rallies, and holding speaking engagements to raise awareness among my peers. We are building TTG chapters across the country with the help of our national partnerships with Whole Foods Market and Pottery Barn Teen, with whom we are planning Project Green Prom. We have been getting new members coming to us from all over the country via our posts on blogs, Web sites, word of mouth, and from the in-store displays at Whole

Foods. Three chapters started up this week . . . it's all pretty amazing to see the campaign gaining lots of great momentum.

When schools or groups of students start a chapter, they receive a tool kit and a mentor who has been involved in our campaign. Teens, moms, teachers, and community members attend our events, which are held regularly wherever we have chapters. So far, we've launched chapters in northern California, New York, Austin, Dallas, Denver, and Houston, and next is Los Angeles. Every school we visit is so excited to join. It is a very contagious, energetic, passionate, and life-changing campaign.

TTG has also had the opportunity to join forces with the world's leading green beauty experts and create a board of advisers, which includes top chemists, product formulators, and the wisdom of resources like the Environmental Working Group's (EWG) Skin Deep Report (www.cosmeticsdatabase.com). EWG's Skin Deep Report evaluates ingredients in more than thirty-seven thousand products, making it the largest data resource of its kind. This gives consumers a place to go to see how harmful the chemicals in their products actually are.

THERE ARE ALTERNATIVES TO CHEMICALS

We at TTG have worked to create *The Dirty Thirty*, an easy-to-use resource that lists chemicals you should avoid in your daily-use products. Developed in partnership with chemists, this reference tool includes chemical names, where they are found, and their purposes and potential harmful factors. TTG has also compiled *Greener Alternatives*, a head-to-toe list of companies and products that have

DIRTY THIRTY

CHEMICALS TO AVOID FOUND IN THE PR

CHEMICAL: ALUMINUM ZIRCONIUM and OTHER ALUMINUM COMPOUNDS
Function: Used to control sweat and odor in the underarms by slowing down the production of sweat.
Present in: Antiperspirants. Banned by EU.
Health concerns: Linked to the development of Alzheimer's Disease; may be linked to breast cancer; probable neurotoxin; respiratory and developmental toxin.

CHEMICAL: BENZYL ACETATE
Function: Solvent; hidden within "fragrance."
Present in: Many cosmetics and personal care products; read labels.
Health concerns: Linked to pancreatic cancer; easily absorbs into skin causing quick systemic effects; animal studies show liver; possible pneumonitis, possible gastrointestinal, liver, and respiratory toxicant.

CHEMICAL: BENZALKONIUM CHLORIDE and BENZETHONIUM CHLORIDE
Function: Antimicrobial agent, deodorant, preservative, biocide relief. Restricted in Japan and Canada.
Present in: Moisturizer, sunscreen, facial cleaner, acne treatment, pain organ system toxicant; animal studies show endocrine disruption and long
Health concerns: Immune system toxicant, may trigger asthma, possible nervous system, respiratory and blood effects; possible carcinogen.

CHEMICAL: BRONOPOL
Function: Preservative.
Present in: Moisturizer, body wash, facial cleaner, makeup remover anti-aging products. Restricted in Canada.
Health concerns: Immune system toxicant, lung and skin toxicant studies show endocrine disruption and gastrointestinal, brain and res system effects; irritant.

CHEMICAL: BUTYL ACETATE
Function: Solvent in polishes and treatments, prevents chipping.
Present in: Nail polish and nail treatments.
Health concerns: Repeated exposure causes skin dryness and cracking; vapors may induce drowsiness or dizziness; flammable.

CHEMICAL: BUTYLATED HYDROXYTO (BHT)/ BUTYLATED HYDROXYANISO
Present in: Many cosmetics and personal care products; foods; change in color.
Banned in EU.
Health Concerns: Immune system toxicant, human carcinogen; animal studies show liver, thyroid and human carcinogen toxicant.

CHEMICAL: ETHOXYLATED INGREDIENTS: CETEARETH/PEG
Present in: Many cosmetics products including shampoo, sunscreen.
Health concerns: Animal studies show sense organs toxicant, also and respiratory toxicant.

COAL TAR

Mia Wasilevich

Environista Extraordinaire

While Erin has never used anything but green deodorant, Mia Wasilevich grew up using conventional beauty products and really wanted to make a change.

Mia Wasilevich, a self-titled Environista Extraordinaire, is a writer and publicist in Los Angeles and an all-around green gal about town. She first became interested in going green when she was twenty-two years old and she realized that her family had begun to develop health issues that had never before appeared in the family tree. She did some sleuthing about products and foods she used on a regular basis and was shocked to find so many toxins in her daily beauty regime. Her advice to all aspiring environistas is to start with something that has an immediate impact and that really means something to you, however trivial it may seem. Changing your deodorant is a great first green step.

Why Are Many of Our Conventional Deodorants Bad?

Location, location, location. We have lymph nodes in our armpits, and these tiny organs serve as filters or traps for foreign and potentially harmful chemicals and help support our immune systems. The aluminum and other chemicals found in deodorants shrink the pores and react with the electrolytes in the sweat to form a gel plug in our sweat glands and slow down the production of sweat. It isn't a natural function of your glands to block the sweat and oils that are supposed to come out. As a result, you compromise your glands and lymphatic areas by congesting them as well as taking in toxic chemicals from the product itself.

So What Can We Do?

I'm a green girl, but I'm not living with B.O. The good news is that there is an alternative. It may take a little time, but it's worth the change. You will have to wean yourself off your conventional deodorant and let your body be cleansed of all those toxins. But once you do this, you'll find that you won't actually need to wear antiperspirant because your body will regulate back to its normal function and cycle. You can then use an all-natural, nontoxic deodorant, as opposed to antiperspirant.

Nancy Redd

Motivational Speaker and Author

While Erin and Mia discovered green replacements for their daily beauty regimes, Nancy Redd went on a quest to find eco-friendly alternatives for her monthly cycle.

Nancy Redd writes about green beauty on the inside and out. She is the *New York Times* bestselling author of *Body Drama*, a book empowering a new generation of women with the gift of self-knowledge. Nancy is also a contributing editor at *CosmoGIRL!* magazine, a self-esteem adviser to *Fitness* magazine, an AOL wellness coach, and an editor for the MSN Dove campaign and www.planetgreen.discovery.com.

Green Your Period

The average woman will have nearly five hundred periods in her lifetime and may use as many as 16,800 tampons! Landfills and sewage systems are overflowing with an estimated 20 billion pads and tampons in North America alone. Thinking about how my own monthly cycle contributes to those alarming statistics, I was encouraged to find out that there were green alternatives—from reusable tampons to reusable pads—on the market. Check out Web sites like www.gladrags.com and www.manymoonsalternatives.com to see if there is a product that can work for you.

www.gladrags.com

www.manymoonsalternatives.com

been vetted by campaign members for safety, sustainability, and practicality. If products are not safe for our bodies, chances are the processes by which they are made and disposed of are far from harmless to the environment. TTG seeks to support companies that take into consideration not only formulation and ingredients, but also business practices that respect the environment, fair-trade labor policies, community empowerment, sustainable packaging (biodegradable packing peanuts and planter boxes, for example), and the cradle-to-cradle approach toward an endless cycle without waste.

Through TTG, I've learned about the many environmentally friendly and health-conscious companies that are out there. Not only are their beauty products entirely free of synthetic chemicals, potential carcinogens, toxins, and pesticides, but they are actually more effective and nourishing for the entire body. I was ecstatic to hear that there is a way to have pure and natural beauty essentials *plus* a plump crimson pout and toxin-free smoky lavender eyes!

TAKING TEENS TURNING GREEN TO THE TOP— THE CREATION OF THE TEENS TURNING GREEN COLLECTION

Seeing all these green products encouraged us to develop TTG's own body-care line. We launched the Teens Turning Green Collection in 2008, and it is sold exclusively at Whole Foods Markets nationwide. This is the first eco-friendly body-care line created

"GREEN" YOUR PROM

FOR SHAILENE WOODLEY, STAR OF *THE SECRET LIFE OF THE AMERICAN TEENAGER*, GOING GREEN MEANS GIVING YOUR PROM AN ECO-FRIENDLY MAKEOVER!

In the rush to find the perfect date, the perfect dress, and the perfect dinner spot, it's easy to forget the impact you're having on the environment when you're preparing for prom night. My tip to you is to take a moment and think about how you can "green" your prom-night plans—it's a lot easier than you think!

For example, ditch the limo and use a more gas-efficient vehicle to carpool with friends to the dance. Also, make an impression by wearing a stylish vintage dress rather than buying a new one, and use organic and locally grown flowers for your date's boutonniere. For dinner, make an all-organic, locally grown meal with your prom group at home before hitting the town! And encourage your school's prom committee to make "green" decisions when they're planning for the big night, too!

Shailene Woodley

by teens for teens! The products are made with the safest ingredients and incorporate sustainable packaging with eco-mindful business practices. These products are memorable, with great scents and textures, and above all, they *really* work! All items also adhere to the Whole Foods Personal Body Care Standard, the most rigorous of standards in retail. And 10 percent of profits after expenses are donated back to Teens Turning Green.

www.wholefoodsmarket.com

SB 1712 MIGDEN
ADULTERATED COSMETICS
California State Assembly

WHAT'S NEXT FOR THE FUTURE?

The fight for safe personal-care products unfortunately won't go away anytime soon. We still need people to stand up for the right to have safe cosmetics and beauty products. I hope to continue my work with Teens Turning Green and focus on the promotion of our new body-care line. And I continue to visit government offices and testify on the issue of toxins in personal-care products. I am looking forward to continuing to work with other teens to ensure a healthy body, planet, and future for this generation and beyond. I believe that together we can make a beautiful and healthy world for our children and children's children. We are a generation of change makers, and we are here to stay!

 Erin's TIP

Transition to safer and healthier beauty products gradually; don't just throw away everything you have now. As you finish your conventional products, replace each with a greener alternative. Not only is this much less wasteful, but it also does not require you to spend a ton of money all at once. Focus on the four daily essentials: soap, shampoo, deodorant, and toothpaste.

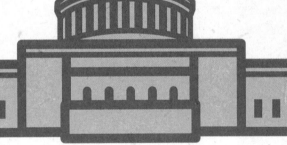

Lunch Bags
for a Cause

Adrienne
Boukis

Age: 13
Hometown:
Walnut Creek, California

MEET ADRIENNE AND HER CAUSE

I'm Adrienne Boukis, and I'm thirteen. I go to middle school in Walnut Creek, California. I usually think of myself as a teenager, a soccer player, a scholarly student, and a good citizen. I'm a big sister to Mackenzie, who is three years younger than me, and I'm an active member of my Girl Scout troop, a group that includes my best friends in the world. When I think about my future, I know that I have the potential to become anything I want.

In middle school, we eat lunch in our cafeteria. Lots of kids bring their lunches to school in brown paper bags. When I started realizing that a lot of bags pile up in the trash bins at lunchtime, I was surprised. You don't have to be a math genius to realize that with so many students having lunch at so many schools across the country, that mounting pile of daily trash is not so good for our planet. And, more important, it is a completely avoidable problem.

I did not set out to become an activist for the environment. I just got tired of seeing piles of dirty paper lunch bags littering my school. I guess you could say it was my call to action, something that felt like an undeniable urge to fix things and make them right. And usually when I want to get something done, I just do it! I figure out the problem, determine how to fix it, and never hesitate to ask for help along the way. In this case, I found my best helpers right at home.

One day, I came home from school

looking for a small bag that I could reuse every day to carry my lunch. In my middle school, we didn't have lockers. I didn't want to carry around a lunch box or anything bulky, so I brought my lunch to school in a brown paper bag, just like everyone else. I used the paper bags as many times as I could, but they would get wet and sticky after a few days. It was pretty gross. But it bugged me every time I threw away a brown paper bag because I knew it was wasteful. I asked my mom if there was something she had that I could use instead. We looked around and didn't find anything that seemed right. Everything was either too big or too small, or was lined with bulky insulation, which is not environmentally friendly. The linings are made out of synthetic materials like plastic or aluminum, the kinds of materials that will sit in landfills for many years if thrown out. I just wanted something simple that I could put in my back pocket or in my backpack after I ate my lunch. Basically, I wanted the equivalent of a washable brown paper bag.

WHAT DID ADRIENNE DO ABOUT IT?

We looked everywhere, but a washable brown paper bag just didn't exist. So I asked my mom to help me create one. She made me a lunch bag out of recycled fabric, and I used it for my whole sixth-grade year. It was a little weird-looking, kind of uneven around the edges, and the corners were a bit scrunched, but I liked it and I used it. It wasn't perfect because the cloth

would get stinky and lose its shape, but it still did the trick. As I was getting my school supplies together for the new school year, that old lunch bag had definitely seen better days and had to be retired. While I really hate throwing anything away, I needed a cool replacement.

I could picture my dream bag in my head, and so I sat down and sketched it out. It had to be the same dimensions as a standard paper lunch bag, and it had to be biodegradable, a big improvement over my lumpy sixth-grade cloth bag. My mom took a look at it and helped me measure out a pattern. We came up with a design for a bag that was amazing. It really did look almost exactly like a paper lunch bag. It's half the size of binder paper, and fits in your pocket easily. And it has handles and a little Velcro closure at the top. We found a special biodegradable fabric that is made of 30 percent postconsumer product (which comes from recycled plastic bottles) and is available in lots of colors. It's washable and can be recycled when you are done with it because it decomposes very quickly in compost or landfill. Just like that, we cut and sewed the bag, and the next day I was carrying my lunch in my dream bag to the first day of school.

At lunch, my friends asked me where they could buy a lunch bag like mine. So when I came back home, I told my mother that we had to make more bags. If I got my friends to use these bags, then we could help the Earth by saving some trees. Luckily, my mom knew someone through her job who runs a factory that could make multiple reproductions of my dream lunch bag. I figured that if I liked it and my friends liked it, there would

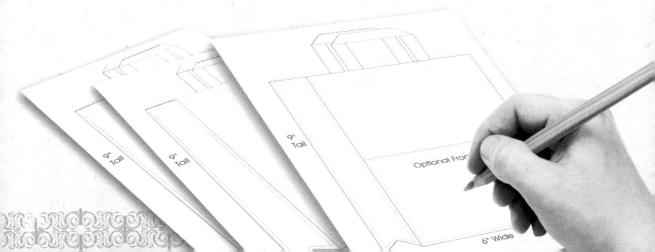

be other kids who might like it, too. Suddenly, I had a vision of kids all over the country carrying their lunch in my "green" bags instead of in wasteful paper bags, and those piles of lunchtime trash would quickly start to shrink. My mom talked to the factory and set the wheels in motion, and all of a sudden, we found ourselves in the green bag business!

WHAT HAPPENED NEXT?

When the bags came in, I asked my Girl Scout troop to serve as my "research-and-development team" and test the bags, then give me some honest feedback. They carried the bags to school for a week, throwing them around the playground, stretching them to the fullest with the food they packed for lunch, and then putting them through the wringer, literally, by repeated machine washing cycles. When they reported back to me, it was a unanimously positive vote of confidence. They absolutely loved the bags! What was even cooler was that the girls in my troop started decorating the bags with fabric pens and jewels. Everyone personalized her bag so we wouldn't get them mixed up at school, and each bag was unique because we had designed them ourselves!

Overnight, there was a great demand in our town for my bags. Neighbors began knocking on my door with orders, and a grocery store asked if they could sell them at their cashier stands. My aunt runs a race every year in Colorado, and she told me that they always give out lunch bags filled with healthy snacks after people finish the race. I sent the race organizers a few sample bags, which they liked so much that they bought three thousand to deliver lunches to all the runners. And the bags' popularity didn't stop there. Through DisneyFamily.com, I entered an online contest to send in your best "green" ideas. Out of more than eight hundred entries, DisneyFamily.com listed six of their favorite green ideas for 2008, and my bag was one of them! Suddenly, my little homespun lunch bag was the hotly sought-after "it" bag!

USING THE BAGS FOR MORE THAN JUST LUNCH

My bags turned out to be so much more than just a green-friendly fashion statement. My sister Mackenzie used the bags to raise money at her school. Parents and kids scooped them up, and within minutes, she had sold fifty bags! It felt good to know that my bags were being put to all kinds of good uses.

But I knew there was more that I could do. I was learning quite a lot about the importance of helping others in a class I was taking called Teens Around the World, which highlighted problems facing teenagers in other parts of the world. I learned about issues of human rights, fair trade, and economic disparity. I was very grateful to be blessed with the comfort and security afforded by my family and country, but I was distressed to learn about boys and girls suffering from hunger and injustice. I wanted to help. It all came together for me in May 2008 when a cyclone struck Myanmar, followed

by a devastating earthquake in China, and there was a call to action to send aid to the region. I realized that my bags could be used as a philanthropic tool, a fund-raiser to quickly pull together donations for Myanmar. I set up a stand at school and in only two hours, I sold enough bags to send $1,000 to the nonprofit organization Save the Children. The bags were helping people and the environment at the same time!

A reporter wrote about the fund-raiser in the local paper and then a newswire picked up the story, and orders have been pouring in for my bags ever since. There were times when my mom was worried that we would be the only people who would use the bags and that it was risky to order production of so many of them because people might not buy the five thousand bags she'd produced. I knew in my heart that that was not going to be the case and pushed my mom to keep the production line going. She is now very confident that this is the right thing to do for the environment *and* a great fund-raising project for other schools. And with all the orders coming in, our biggest problem is keeping up with the demand! You can order my bags online at www.greengearbag.com or download an order form on the site and send it to me.

Welcome to Green Gear Bags.
HOME
Place Order
F.A.Q.
The Story
Contact Us

www.greengearbag.com

WHAT'S NEXT FOR THE FUTURE?

I think even bigger things lie ahead for my bags. My long-term goal is to get my bags into national grocery stores. I want them to be as normal as a brown paper bag and available to everyone. My other goal is to get my bags to other schools so they can have them and use them for fund-raisers as well.

Mackenzie worries about global warming and animals becoming extinct. I often remind her that part of the solution is trying to think about your actions every day. As an older sister, it's important for me to set a good example for her to follow, even though we are so different. I turn off the lights when I leave a room, recycle bottles and cans, and turn off the water while I'm brushing my teeth. It's also a bigger joint effort of my whole family. We have solar panels on our roof, and a compost bin in our backyard, and Mackenzie and I help in the garden by growing our own vegetables. We also carpool to school, and our family

tries to reuse or give things away instead of throwing things in the trash. I would advise other girls to look around to see what they can do to make a difference. It doesn't have to be anything big; we all just have to try to do small things every day.

 ## Adrienne's TIP

The average American consumer uses between five hundred and a thousand plastic bags every year. That's approximately *100 billion* bags, and we recycle only 2 percent of them. When you go to the mall, bring your own bags! Get some plain canvas bags and have a decorating party with your friends. That way, you'll have your own "signature" bag every time you go shopping.

Green Fashionista

Maya Moverman

Age: 14
Hometown:
New York,
New York

MEET MAYA AND HER CAUSE

I'm Maya Moverman, and I'm fourteen years old. I live in New York City, which I love! In my spare time, I like to read, write, do anything artistic, listen to music, watch movies, and hang out with my friends and family. And although I love to shop, I've found that the best bargains are right here at home in my own closet because green fashion is my passion.

In my science class last year, my teacher explained to us that global warming was threatening our planet. I had always done my part by recycling and not littering, but after hearing the facts of global warming, I decided I needed to do more. How was I as a clothing consumer contributing to the environmental crisis? Could the fashion industry be a culprit? With so many manufacturing facilities at work constantly churning out new clothing, I hated to think that my favorite garments were made at the cost of our clean air.

I was very concerned and began calculating the carbon footprint of an average outfit I wear. My ballet flats were made in Italy, my pleated skirt in China, my tights are German, and my T-shirt came from Los Angeles. It took a lot of boats, planes, trains, and automobiles to pull this outfit together, and that translates to a whole lot of air pollution. And then I started adding up all those outfits I've outgrown or no longer love that have been thrown out. All my old clothes taking up all that space in a landfill for years upon years—that's a huge amount of pollution. It made me think about all the other stuff sitting in my drawers or hanging in my closet. I realized that it's far greener to shop at home, and all it would take are a needle, some thread, and a little imagination.

Alexx Levin-Monkarsh

Eco Clothing Designer, Alexx Jae for Environmental Media Association (EMA)

Maya aspires to be a green girl designer just like Alexx Levin-Monkarsh, for whom green is much more than just a color.

After college, Alexx began her career working for celebrity favorite PRIMP's cutting-edge designer Wells Butler on a line of comfortable yet girlishly stylish clothing. When she decided to start creating her own pieces, Alexx wanted

to find a way to combine her love of design with her passion for the environment. She turned to her mother, Debbie Levin, President of the Environmental Media Association, and they collaborated to produce a fashion line that

takes "organic" to a whole new level by using sustainable fabric and bearing slogans like "Where'syourhybrid?" and "Compactfluorescents are sexy." Celebs like Anna Faris and Christina Aguilera have turned "green" for her pieces, and it hasn't stopped there. Even Nicole Richie and Heidi Klum have picked up Alexx's bamboo duds for their tots. Clothes can be purchased on www.ema-online.org, and all profits from sales are donated to EMA to help fund environmental education. While Alexx is dedicated to designing fabulous clothes, she is first and foremost a devoted leader of fashion's environmentally friendly revolution.

Alexx's Tip

To be truly green, you have to think about the whole process of how a particular fabric came to be, where it's been, and where it's going. When shopping, look for sustainable fabrics, like bamboo. It's a natural fiber that comes from the pulp of bamboo grass, which is quick-growing and easily replaced. When processed, it becomes soft, fast-drying, and hypoallergenic, and it contains a natural antibacterial that kills odors.

MAYA TRANSFORMS HER OLD CLOTHES

I opened my closet and looked at my old clothes in a completely different way. Recycling and refashioning your clothes into unique new outfits is an easy and fun way to reduce waste, conserve our natural resources, and protect the air we breathe. So I dusted off my grandmother's old sewing machine, a beloved hand-me-down, took the sewing skills I learned from my art teacher, and got to work designing a whole new wardrobe out of old stuff. I created some fabulous pieces that were at once super-retro and fresh. For me, this is serious green fun.

And there is more I can do. I recently hosted a Recycle Your Clothes party, which is something you can do with your friends. Everyone brings a few old pieces of clothing to put in the collection, and then we review what we have on hand and discuss all the possible designs. Old jeans can be made into a funky purse, a T-shirt can get a new life with old buttons or trim, and dad's old neckties can even be transformed into a cute mini! Next, we cut and sew together all kinds of new outfits. Of course, it's important to end the night with a spectacular fashion show!

EARTH-FRIENDLY FASHION TAKEN TO THE NEXT LEVEL

Recycling your clothes is not the only way to be Earth-conscious when it comes to fashion. If you want to buy new clothes as well as refashion old ones, you should look for Earth-friendly materials like organic cotton, hemp, wool, soy silk, and bamboo. You can also hit up your local thrift store for those one-of-a-kind vintage pieces. After you have outgrown your clothes, it is important not to contribute to the trash that has piled up in our landfills. You can help others by donating to a local homeless shelter or charities such as Goodwill and the Salvation Army.

WHAT'S NEXT FOR THE FUTURE?

My personal goal in the near future is to develop and grow as an eco-conscious fashion designer. I plan to continue recycling and refashioning my clothes into new and fabulous designs as well as work in other creative and fun ways to help the environment!

Maya's TIP

- Your recycled designs can make fabulous gifts for birthdays and holidays. I recommend designing the gift to fit your friend's unique personality.
- You've outgrown your recycled designs . . . what to do next? Pass them on to a younger sibling, and she can add her own style to the piece. If you don't have any other girls in your family, you can cut up the recycled outfit and add the pieces to another fabulous design!

Caitlin Brunell

Founder of Caitlin's Closet

Meet Caitlin and Her Cause

I'm Caitlin Brunell, and I'm sixteen years old. If you are anything like me, you have been dreaming for most of your young-adult life about your high school prom and that very important prom dress. But it can be hard to find a dress for prom or other special occasions that you love, that's decently priced, and that's eco-friendly. Feeling good about

yourself comes from within; however, feeling good about your dress gives you the confidence to conquer the world! That's what I was thinking when I formed Caitlin's Closet, a nonprofit organization that collects gently used special-occasion dresses and distributes them to girls all over the country. By reusing our dresses, we are helping the environment, saving tons of energy that would otherwise go into manufacturing new dresses.

Since its founding in 2006, Caitlin's Closet has collected more than five thousand prom gowns and special-occasion dresses! Partnering with Children's Services in Washington, D.C., and Old Dominion High School in Sterling, Virginia, I was able to give more than eighty girls the chance to attend their proms last spring feeling and looking like the belle of the ball.

My work with Caitlin's Closet helped me to be crowned Miss America's Outstanding Teen 2008, representing the Commonwealth of Virginia. I also won more than $30,000 in college scholarships at the Miss America's Outstanding Teen competition! It has been an amazing year, and in the future I look forward to helping many more girls look and feel fabulous.

There are many ways you can help, too. You can host dress drives or Caitlin's Closet events in your hometown or donate your own dresses to us. Check out our Web site, www.caitlinscloset.org, for all the details.

For longtime friends *Odessa Whitmire, Summer Phoenix,* and *Ruby Canner,* being green means making timeless clothing from forgotten textiles.

www.someoddrubies.com

We share a love of vintage clothing, so the idea of collaborating on a line that reconstructed beautiful designs and materials from the past for discerning fashionistas of today was a natural progression. With no classic training, we had a vision for "Some Odd Rubies" and simultaneously launched both our collection and flagship store in the spring of 2003.

The line was a hit, as was our store, and we were encouraged to bring our sensibility out west; in 2006 Los Angeles welcomed the opening of a second boutique. Our one-of-a-kind designs aim to bring out the effortless beauty within each unique woman.

OUR TIP TO YOU: Check your closet for old jeans and stained tees. Try dyeing them a cool color or bleach splattering for a fresh new look! Sometimes we do both! It's an easy way to hide the flaws of those forgotten threads, and it's recycling!

Check out our Web site, www.someoddrubies.com, to find out who carries our clothing near you, or drop by one of our boutiques: 151 Ludlow Street, NY, NY 10002 or 8024 West Third Street, Los Angeles, CA 90024.

The Women of the Roxy Greenprints Design Team

GreenPRINT The Roxy Greenprints Design Team designs the eco-friendly clothes that make up the Greenprints brand. For this team, Greenprints stands for more than just products. It's about a way of life in which every girl does her part in helping the environment by making smart, sustainable fashion choices!

The Women of Roxy's Tip—Dress Green

Be an informed consumer when you are picking out that next fashionable outfit to wear at school, on the slopes, or in the water! Traditional methods of making clothes often have a negative impact on the environment through the use of harmful pesticides and dyes. Support brands that are taking steps to become more eco-friendly. Roxy Greenprints is one brand that is doing just that. Get the details and get involved at www.roxy.com.

www.roxy.com

CHAPTER 2

THE ANIMAL ADVOCATES

Manatee Minder

Stephanie Cohen

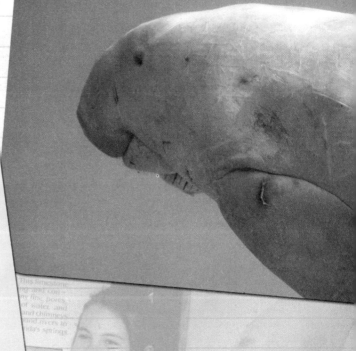

Age: 16
Hometown:
Dallas-Fort Worth, Texas

MEET STEPHANIE AND HER CAUSE

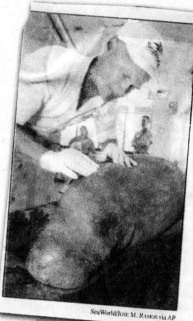

My name is Stephanie Cohen, I'm sixteen years old, and I live in Texas with my mother, father, and brother, as well as my beloved rescued Chihuahua, Paris. Rescuing animals is my passion, and one that I share with my family. Our household is a menagerie of rescued pets, including dogs, horses, guinea pigs, mice, and even a bearded lizard from Australia. If we can't keep the abandoned animals ourselves, we help place them in new homes. I'm also just as concerned about taking care of animal species that are endangered because humans are encroaching on their natural habitats. It makes me so angry to think that sometimes people just don't understand how their behavior impacts the animals with which we share our oceans, land, and skies. I have made it my personal mission to champion wildlife and domestic animals. But there's one animal in particular that really inspired my activism.

When I was in the second grade, my neighbor brought over a news article about an injured baby manatee that really captured my heart. Although I live in the Dallas–Fort Worth area, landlocked in the middle of Texas, and there aren't any manatees swimming around my town, my neighbor knew that I liked to visit the two manatees at the Dallas Aquarium. I read the newspaper article about that injured baby manatee over and over again. The manatee had been hit by a boat and found in Eddy Creek at the Canaveral National Seashore in Florida. Thankfully, the marine biologists at SeaWorld had saved the little guy, and he was on the road to recovery at the marine park. But I became absolutely fascinated by this odd and some- what alien-looking creature.

THE PLIGHT OF THE MANATEE

After reading about the injured manatee, I felt that I needed to do something to help these creatures. My local librarian helped me find a few resource books, and I found a lot of informa- tion on the Internet, especially on the SeaWorld Web site. Manatees, or sea cows, are mammals related to elephants. These slow-moving vege- tarians eat about 10 to 15 percent of their body weight per day, which equals 100 to 150 pounds of underwater vegetation, as they can weigh more than a thousand pounds and grow to more than twelve feet. They generally live along the Florida coastline. They for- age around for food and then come up for air about every five minutes, and that's when they are at risk. With more and more people enjoying boating, these friendly animals are getting cut up by the propeller blades on motorboats.

When I read this, I could not stop thinking about that poor manatee in the article. In 2003, manatees became an endangered species, mostly due to the increased number of people enjoying water sports and building marinas in the manatees' habitat. The prob- lem was that this animal had no voice.

Similar to how polar bears are threatened by the man-made pollution that is causing global warming and melting their ice floe habitats, manatees are being killed by the growing number of humans buzzing carelessly across the surface of their underwater habitats. Naturally curious and mellow, manatees are not afraid of humans. This is partly why they get hurt so often. Manatees are in peril because of human impact, and it is up to humans to take action on their behalf to save them. If I could make people aware of the consequences of their reckless behavior, I could save manatees.

HOW STEPHANIE MADE A DIFFERENCE

SeaWorld's Dr. Scott Gearhart, the veterinarian who was interviewed for the article my neighbor brought by, said that they needed funds to cover the continued medical care of the recovering baby manatee. I decided to raise some money to help. I asked our own family vet if I could put a collection jar in his waiting room, and he readily agreed. I posted general information about manatees and the original article next to the jar. And in one day, I collected $27. Not bad for a second-grader! I then wrote a letter to Dr. Gearhart, who was still taking care of the wounded manatee, and enclosed the check for $27 as a donation. In the letter, I explained that I wanted to help that manatee get better so they could release it back into the wild.

A few weeks later, I received a phone call from Dr. Gearhart thanking me for the donation. He told me about Hubbs-SeaWorld Research Institute, the nonprofit part of SeaWorld (www.hswri .org). They invited me to come visit them in Orlando, and that's when I met the injured baby manatee close up. It was so sweet! That was more than eight years ago, and ever since then, I've been helping the organization by sending supplies and money.

STEPHANIE'S HUMANITARIAN EFFORTS

Collecting money from my vet's office was just the beginning. I've had the most success raising funds by selling homemade manatee pins. My mom is really good at arts and crafts, so when I sketched a drawing of a pin I wanted to make, she helped me make a few samples out of clay. I sold the first batch to my family and close friends. People reacted to them so positively that I produced more and sold them at public events, including school games and fairs, garage sales, charity drives, animal shelters, Earth Day celebrations, and other community gatherings. The pins are a fantastic way to raise money and public awareness for these gentle giants. Each pin was affixed to a handmade card that explained the plight of the manatees, and I signed each pin I made. I can't begin to express the joy I felt when I could look over at a huge crowd of people and see my little manatee pins everywhere! I knew I was making a difference. When I received a call from Dr. Gearhart a year later to let me know that his center had fully rehabilitated the baby manatee and that they had sent him back into the wild, I was ecstatic. It felt so good to have been a part of that effort, but I knew many other manatees remained in peril. There was much more work to be done.

My second-grade teacher took an interest in my devotion to the cause of the manatees and mentored me. I was pretty shy at first and didn't

like to speak in front of a class or a crowd. But it's hard to get people's attention if you aren't willing to talk to them! My mentor encouraged me to do my school projects about manatees, and, over the years between second grade and sixth grade, I became an expert on the subject. My confidence grew, and soon I was presenting my projects to everyone, eventually teaching a whole class about manatees. My mentor had helped me overcome my shyness and find my own voice. And with my ever-expanding knowledge and newfound confidence, I became a voice for the manatees.

When I reached the sixth grade, I found a new supporter in my sixth-grade teacher, who helped me with a very ambitious independent project—something I thought could bring awareness of manatees to many people. I came up with the idea of generating a long paper chain of love and public support for the manatees. My "HuManatee" chain would actually serve as a petition asking state politicians to enact laws and regulations that would protect these gentle creatures. I asked my classmates, school faculty, neighbors, and community members to sign their names along with a little message of support on narrow strips of gray paper, and I linked all the signatures together into a paper chain that was thirty-six feet long! I then sent the chain to the governor of Florida,

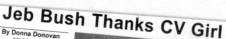

Jeb Bush Thanks CV Girl

By Donna Donovan
STAFF WRITER

When Stephanie Cohen received a donation request from a Manatee rescue group three years ago, she started a local campaign of her own to help preserve these endangered mammals.

What followed next, was a surprising chain of events that included setting up her own non-profit organization, called Kids Making a Difference, taking a sponsored trip to Orlando, Fla., courtesy of the Hubbs Research facility at Sea World, and receiving a letter from Florida Gov. Jeb Bush.

Stephanie sent the governor a letter in October suggesting that boats be outfitted with wire cages to protect aquatic animals from propeller blades. The blades are killing and maiming scores of manatees.

The following excerpts were taken from Bush's Nov. 10 letter:

"I appreciate your sharing your thoughts about this endangered species, and for sharing your idea for a propeller guard.

"Manatee 'safe zones' have been set up all over the state, and the [Florida Fish and Wildlife Conservation Commission] has a program to teach boaters and others how to avoid hurting this amazing animal.

"I promise to do my best to protect our environment and will continue efforts to increase the population and well-being of manatees."

The governor also wished

Caption: Stephanie Cohen (l) and Cross Timbers Middle School science teacher Mary Potysman, are draped in the paper chain representing donors who have contributed to Stephanie's fundraising drive to save the Florida manatees from extinction. - Staff photo

Stephanie "good luck with your company, Kids Making a Difference."

Stephanie, 11, is the daughter of Karen and Dr. Michael Cohen of Colleyville. She has a brother, Connor, 8, and attends Cross Timbers Middle School in Grapevine. Her pets include three dogs, three guinea pigs, a lizard, a rabbit and fish.

She doesn't have a manatee, but she has seen one up close.

"In 2001, Sea World sent me down to meet the manatees and the people who capture them," Stephanie recalled. "I was on the

See MANATEE, Page 5

Jeb Bush, with a letter explaining that people in Texas care about manatees and wanted him to take action on their behalf for manatees' continued protection. I proposed that all boats be required to fit wire cages around their propellers to save manatees from injury and death. I sent this with the understanding that my voice could go unheard, but I was excited when the governor wrote back to me! He thanked me for sharing my idea and told me about the program the Florida Fish and Wildlife Conservation Commission was running to set up Manatee Safe Zones all over the state. They were working to educate boaters and others on how to avoid hurting this amazing animal.

STEPHANIE STARTS THE ORGANIZATION KIDS MAKING A DIFFERENCE

My paper-chain-link petition received some attention in regional and national media and from kids across the country. They started asking me how they might get involved with my animal conservation work. I was only eleven years old, yet kids everywhere were looking to me for advice on how they could make a difference. There were many other animals needing help and so many kids wanting to do something that I decided to expand my efforts. In 2003, with the help of my aunt and my mother, I formed the organization Kids Making a Difference (KMAD).

www.kmad.org

Today, KMAD is an award-winning, nationally recognized nonprofit organization. We bring together
youth from across the country who want to help animals and have a positive influence on the world. Through
the organization and my Web site, www.kmad.org, kids
are supporting other kids with ideas and resources to
make an impact in their communities. Under adult volunteer supervision, we are making positive strides
by collecting needed items for homeless pets and
fund-raising for the preservation of endangered
wildlife. We actively seek out people who need our
help, and on several occasions have come to the aid
of animal shelters hit by natural disasters. And in the last
five years, the organization has logged more than six hundred volunteer hours perform-
ing community service and fund-raising on behalf of animal causes. While "Saving Our
World One Animal at a Time," we are growing up to be young adults of great compassion
and inner strength.

MONEY FOR MANATEES

Fund-raising is my most important activity, and I'm doing it
all the time via www.kmad.org, through eBay's online charity
auctions, with garage sales, and by selling manatee Christmas ornaments, manatee candles, and manatee cards. I'm
very proud of the considerable amount of supplies we've sent to
Hubbs-SeaWorld for manatee conservation. At my events, I always
put up a pledge board and ask kids to write on leaf-shaped paper
what they are willing to do to help the environment. They pin their
promises onto our Tree of Pledges, and it's very rewarding
to see how those promises are filling in the branches and
turning the people in my community green.

My latest fund-raising idea is the "HuManatee" quilt. I plan to auction it off to raise money to buy a truck for Hubbs–SeaWorld Research Institute's Stranding Program. Their truck is old and always getting stuck in the sand when they go out to rescue a stranded dolphin or whale. I've asked celebrities to sign a square, and some of the names I've collected so far include Robin Williams, Matthew Broderick, Nikki Blonsky, Dolly Parton, John Travolta, Bill Cosby, Emeril Lagasse, Martha Stewart, Bob Barker, Alex Trebek, Tim Allen, Arnold Palmer, Rascal Flatts, John McCain, Danica Patrick, Kate Bosworth, and Emmitt Smith!

People are really starting to care about manatees, putting the mandated cages on their boats and being more considerate when entering their habitat. In April 2007, the U.S. Fish and Wildlife Service announced that they would reclassify manatees as "threatened" instead of "endangered." Florida manatees are showing positive growth, having doubled their population since 1991. I believe that my efforts—promoting manatee awareness, educating the public, supporting pro-manatee regulations, and enlisting other young activists to

the cause—have contributed to the improved condition of the species. It's a great feeling to know you've contributed to this! But there is still more work to be done. Manatees are still in danger, and development and boating laws need to be enforced to protect their future.

STEPHANIE WALKS THE WALK BY HELPING OTHER YOUNG ACTIVISTS

Today, I'm more committed than ever to the continued success of my organization. I am still a manatee "maniac" and raise funds, speak to the public, and blog on every possible manatee-related topic. I even started an adopt-a-manatee program for several elementary schools. On any given weekend, you can also find me working with other "kid activists" in a variety of community service activities, like raising money to buy dog beds and other supplies for animal shelters. We currently have more than a hundred active members, at least one from every state, and new applications come in the mail weekly. You can download a free application on my Web site and tell us what interests you. We then use that to connect you with other kids interested in the same causes. If you are under eighteen, we ask that a parent or guardian sign the application.

What started out with just me has grown into a nationwide network of like-minded kid activists. I personally stay in touch with everyone through a monthly newsletter. I like

to share stories of what our members are doing because most of our members are in middle school or high school and are empowered by hearing about the work of their peers. I make a point of supporting the interests and activities of our other members so that they all know their work is important and appreciated.

A FURRY FUTURE

My crusade continues. I feel an obligation to lead my peers in preserving our planet and caring for its other inhabitants. I don't sit on my laurels; instead, I challenge myself to upgrade each achievement. Eight years ago I raised $27 in a day at the vet's office; in 2006, I helped raise $100,000 for the SPCA of Texas in their Strut Your Mutt fund-raising event. (Actually, in that case, I have to give the credit to my dog, Paris, who really did all the strutting.) I have the good fortune of signing a lot of donation checks to worthy causes that KMAD supports. I know I can do more, but to make a real difference on a global scale, I need a solid college education and professional guidance. I am interested in studying animal behavior and following the path of my hero, Dr. Jane Goodall, who has accomplished so much on behalf of wildlife causes and understanding. Although I do think that I'll probably be swapping her jungle attire for a wet suit!

Stephanie's TIP

It is unfortunate that many animals are in danger. Visit your local animal shelter to see how you can help. Encourage adoption and animal rescue! If your interest in animals runs to the more exotic, call your local zoo or the Association of Zoos & Aquariums (www.aza.org) to see if they have youth training programs and internships.

   And check out my Web site, www.kmad.org, for all sorts of ideas on how you can make a difference.

www.aza.org

Dr. Jane Goodall

Founder, The Jane Goodall Institute and Roots & Shoots

Lots of green girls are following in the footsteps of Dr. Jane Goodall, the world-renowned primatologist and conservationist. Although she has received many honors for her environmental and humanitarian work, she is most recognized for her almost fifty-year study of chimpanzee social and family interactions at Gombe National Park in Tanzania. She essentially changed the landscape of scientific research forever when her discovery of chimps making and using tools forced scientists to revise the definition of being human. "Dr. Jane"—as she is known to so many—is deeply committed to helping young leaders make positive change happen. She shares her wisdom and experience in support of all efforts to make the world a better, greener place.

The Jane Goodall Institute (JGI), the organization she founded in 1977, is dedicated to advancing the power of individuals to improve the environment for all living things. While continuing Dr. Jane's efforts to study and protect chimpanzees, JGI has also become a leader in innovative community-centered conservation and development approaches in Africa that better the lives of local people. In 1991, Dr. Jane founded Roots & Shoots, JGI's global environmental and humanitarian youth program. With tens of thousands of young people in almost a hundred countries, the Roots & Shoots network connects youth of all ages who share a desire to create a better world. Young people identify problems in their communities and take action. Roots & Shoots has a proven track record of engaging young people in hands-on projects that benefit people, animals, and the environment.

Dr. Jane is inspirational proof that one committed individual can make a world of difference. And today, at over seventy-five years old, she refuses to retire and spends her time traveling the globe, bringing her message of hope by speaking directly to young people and inspiring new generations to care for the planet. Dr. Jane believes that making a change for the better starts with one person: you!

She says, "Every single one of you can make a difference every day. At the Jane Goodall Institute and at Roots & Shoots, we say, *Think globally, act locally*, because if you start rolling up your sleeves and act locally, it makes a difference. Everybody matters."

Meet some of the grown-up green girls working with Dr. Jane in a variety of JGI programs.

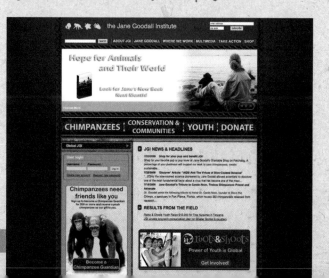

Alice Macharia

JGI Program Manager (East Africa), Africa Programs

I was raised in Kenya and attended college at the University of Nairobi before joining the Jane Goodall Institute as an intern. I became part of the Africa Programs team, working closely with all our programs in East Africa, including Uganda, Tanzania, and Eastern Democratic Republic of the Congo.

Like so many people who live in Kenya, in both cities and rural areas, I had never visited the many wonderful places that tourists come to see in the country, like the Maasai Mara and Tsavo National Park. I realized that it is very important that we, as local people from these countries, understand the importance of the wild animals and plants so that we can work to protect them. As a program manager, I have opportunities to travel to the field to see our programs in action, to work together with our great field staff, and to monitor and provide advice on how to improve our efforts.

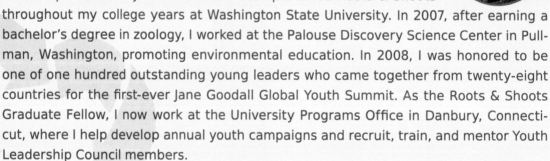

Shanay Healy, 20, Youth Leadership Fellow, Roots & Shoots

When I was sixteen years old, I heard Dr. Jane speak at a zoo and was so inspired that I launched a local version of her ReBirth the Earth: Trees for Tomorrow campaign as my senior project. Over the course of a year, U.S. Roots & Shoots members planted 3,550 trees across the country while raising more than $16,500 to establish five tree nurseries in Tanzania. In 2008, I was chosen to be the Roots & Shoots Youth Leadership Fellow. I have spent this year working at the national office in Arlington, Virginia, acting as a Roots & Shoots spokesperson at events and conferences in Florida and Oregon and even Qatar!

Katia Rossi, 25, Graduate Fellow, Roots & Shoots

I met Dr. Jane by chance on an airplane in 2001. I overheard her explaining Roots & Shoots to the person seated next to her, and that's what inspired me to join her cause. I set up and led Roots & Shoots throughout my college years at Washington State University. In 2007, after earning a bachelor's degree in zoology, I worked at the Palouse Discovery Science Center in Pullman, Washington, promoting environmental education. In 2008, I was honored to be one of one hundred outstanding young leaders who came together from twenty-eight countries for the first-ever Jane Goodall Global Youth Summit. As the Roots & Shoots Graduate Fellow, I now work at the University Programs Office in Danbury, Connecticut, where I help develop annual youth campaigns and recruit, train, and mentor Youth Leadership Council members.

Want to join Roots & Shoots? Please visit www.rootsandshoots.org.

Lisa Pharaoh

JGI Program Manager (West & Central Africa), Africa Programs

After completing my studies in anthropology and primatology, I began an internship at JGI because I wanted to help protect chimpanzees and the irreplaceable habitat in which they live—which is really at the heart of everyone's work here. While chimpanzees once numbered perhaps more than 1 million at the turn of the twentieth century, today it is estimated that there are fewer than three hundred thousand remaining in the wild. A key factor is destruction of habitat—Africa loses more than 10 million acres of forest every year, twice the world's deforestation rate (source: UNEP). Meanwhile, population growth in Africa is faster than any-

where else, with accompanying poverty and lack of basic needs. As program manager, I have the privilege of helping JGI address the needs of human populations in and around forest habitats—the only way to long-lasting, systemic change. Today, I work with JGI to provide technical support for conservation projects in Congo, Guinea, and Sierra Leone. I travel to these countries to monitor and evaluate the projects and assist as needed, although during my six years with the institute I have been most closely involved with our programs in Congo, including helping manage the Tchimpounga Natural Reserve and Chimpanzee Rehabilitation Center.

Want to find out how you can help save the chimps? Please visit www.janegoodall.org to learn about the Chimpanzee Guardianship program.

Megan Nelson

JGI Conservation Education Manager, Africa Programs

I first learned about Roots & Shoots while interning at the Cincinnati Zoo during college. I taught a variety of zoo-sponsored classes, interpreted at zoo exhibits, and presented keeper lectures. One of my favorite parts of the job was bringing animals to grade-school classes. I spent two years as a volunteer for the Roots & Shoots program of the Jane Goodall Institute in Dar es Salaam, Tanzania, and was then

hired to oversee our California regional activities. I love how this program has a combined focus on the environment, animals, and the human community, and how it engages youth to take action. Today, I work with JGI to provide technical support for conservation education projects in Tanzania, Uganda, and Guinea. I get to travel to these countries to monitor and evaluate the projects and work alongside local staff. It is so inspiring to see how the youth today are taking action in their communities, and I am trying to assist in their efforts.

Bronx River Guardian

Elizabeth Severino

Age: 18
Hometown:
New York,
New York

MEET ELIZABETH AND HER CAUSE

My name is Elizabeth Severino, and I'm eighteen years old. My family is originally from the Dominican Republic, but I was born in New York City. About eight years ago we moved to the projects in the South Bronx. Riding my bike around, I saw trash in the streets and overflowing sewers. It seemed like no one cared about where we lived. In further exploring my new neighborhood, I made a trip to the Bronx River with some friends and saw the most beautiful bird with vivid green and black feathers and yellow legs. But sadly, it was perched on top of a mound of trash next to an abandoned car. Imagine my surprise as I continued exploring and found a whole world of wildlife—birds, fish, beavers, and oysters—struggling for survival in the Bronx River. I knew then that I had to take action to help protect the wildlife and help clean the river for these beautiful animals and for the neighborhood to enjoy.

At first, I was overwhelmed by the huge task at hand. As I spoke to my classmates and family members, it seemed that everyone had more important things to do than clean a polluted river. I was discouraged— why couldn't anyone see the beauty in what the river could be? I just didn't know where to start. But with guidance from my high school counselor, I soon learned about some classes I could join to help me fulfill my new purpose.

ROCKING THE BOAT

Biology has always been my favorite subject. And when I got the chance, I signed up for an animal-care class. It was fun learning to classify and care for animals, building habitats in tanks, and using incubators. However, there was something missing. I told my biology teacher that I was interested in finding other ways to learn how to care for animals, and he encouraged me to join programs where I could spend time outdoors learning about animals in their native habitat. After some research, I found a program in the South Bronx called Rocking the Boat, which focuses on boatbuilding and on-water learning. I could spend time on the river monitoring the water and learning about the different species of wildlife that make their home there. The more I learned, the more I saw the need for habitat restoration and environment and wildlife protection from the many sources of pollution that plague a city river.

www.rockingtheboat.org

The Rocking the Boat facility is in the Bronx, and I was living on the other side of the borough. It was a long, hard commute to make after school, but it was worth it! As soon as I got off the bus and walked to the river's edge, I felt my spirits lift. I knew I had a purpose—to help protect the river's wildlife—and I knew I was exactly where I needed to be.

I was so excited to start the program because it was the first time I had a chance to go rowing on a river in New York City. I didn't know that was possible! Finding so much beauty, nature, and life in my neighborhood made me appreciate every bit of it and want to work hard and do whatever I could to protect it and help it thrive.

LIFE AND RESEARCH ON THE RIVER

In order to fully study life on the river, I had to learn some serious maritime skills, like how to row and how to sail. I was a little nervous and made sure my life jacket was on tight before setting out! By going out on boats, we reached areas and collected information that would not have been possible to gather from land. I learned about testing water for salinity, pH, and oxygen, and measuring toxins and oxygen levels. When there are tons of chemicals and metals dropped into the water, the oxygen gets out of balance. Many fish that were in the river before no longer live there because there's not enough oxygen in the water.

We also went fishing for the purpose of studying what we caught. While we were out testing the water, I was shocked to discover all the amazing fish and beautiful birds

living in the South Bronx, right in my own backyard. I learned how to classify birds by their size, special marks, or color of their feet or beaks. I made lists to mark the type of bird, what it was doing, and where we had found it.

In addition to researching birds and fish, we also studied oysters and macro-invertebrates. These are natural barometers of river health and wellness. I was especially lucky to work with New York City's Urban Park Rangers. They maintain an artificial oyster garden at the mouth of the Bronx River, which provides a place where the oysters can come and

make their home. We learned how to create our own oyster garden and were responsible for introducing and monitoring the growth of baby oysters. Oysters are important because as natural filters for pollution, they benefit the environment. One adult oyster can filter up to fifty gallons of water every day! There used to be hundreds of thousands of oysters in the Bronx River, but they began disappearing when people hunted them for their pearls or for food. Because of these restoration efforts, the oyster population is returning, and the overall condition of the river is improving.

Rocking the Boat has relationships with professional scientists at places like the Audubon Society and Lehman College. So the information we collected went into surveys for these institutions, and they in turn used the surveys for their research. The information provides a picture of birdlife along the river: the types of birds seen, how often they are seen, and during what season they appear. This shows if the bird population is thriving or if it is in decline. It was very satisfying to know that I was gaining new skills, helping gather research to restore the river, and having so much fun at the same time!

I also worked with Lehman College to study macroinvertebrates, which are a vital part of the food chain. These tiny creatures provide food for fish, waterfowl, and other animals. Macroinvertebrates are sensitive to environmental stressors and pollution and can provide clues to the health of a river. Part of my job was to learn how to take samples of these tiny bugs by planting nets and retrieving them after a certain amount of time. By measuring the population that had made its home in the nets, we could measure the quality of the river. All these different tests and studies determine what's happening, and what we can do to make it better.

All I could talk about at school was rowing and sailing and all the different animals I was discovering on the river. Soon, my family, friends, and classmates were asking me to take them on the river so that they could see these creatures for themselves. As I took my friends and family on these boat tours, I pointed out different animals and the importance of restoring the river. It was exciting to see that they were interested in learning how they, too, could help protect the river wildlife.

In the last twenty years, the Bronx River has gone from being a cesspool to being one of the best-kept secrets in the Bronx. In some parts it is an oasis where kids can even swim.

But the river is surrounded by factories and is fed by sewer overflow. It's hard to clean something when the things around it are so dirty. I went in thinking that we could restore the Bronx River to the way it was. I learned that perhaps we can never do that, but we can find a balance, understand the special role of each animal and insect, and help protect species from extinction.

WHERE WILL ELIZABETH'S NEXT VOYAGE TAKE HER?

I help out at Rocking the Boat and love to lead community eco-educational rowing sessions of up to a hundred people across this wonderful river that I call home. Whenever I take someone out on their first New York river ride, I am reminded of how I felt the first time I was on the river. I love seeing the light in people's eyes when they discover the beauty of the Bronx River, a wildlife wonderland in the most unlikely corner of the South Bronx. I encourage younger students in my neighborhood to join organizations like Rocking the Boat and to get out on the water if they have the chance—it's a whole other world right in their own backyard in need of protection!

Elizabeth's TIP

Take a closer look at your neighborhood and you may surprise yourself with the discovery of a natural zoo in your surroundings. Even if you live in a city like me, there are animals, insects, and other creatures sharing this habitat, and they all play a part in keeping our environment healthy. Search out and volunteer for a local environmental group and help preserve your habitat for all its residents, big or small!

Take a step outside your comfort zone. If a city girl like me can become a sailor, so can you! Try something new!

Carey Stanton

**Senior Director of
Education and Integrated Marketing,
National Wildlife Federation (NWF)**

Like Stephanie and Elizabeth, grown-up green girl Carey Stanton works hard to protect wildlife and their natural habitats.

Carey Stanton has always wanted to work for the National Wildlife Federation. She loves helping people discover nature. The NWF inspires Americans to protect wildlife for our children's future. Carey has fifteen years of experience designing and implementing award-winning curricula and training programs for NWF and state agencies. "It has become commonplace for children to grow up in cities and suburbs knowing little about the natural world surrounding them." Carey has been recognized for her leadership in the creation of NWF's model leadership development program for urban and minority youth by the U.S. Environmental Protection Agency (EPA) and U.S. Forest Service. Recently, Carey was the principal adviser and faculty for the launch of Al Gore's Climate Project in the United States and Australia, which trained more than a thousand volunteers to give his presentation, the basis for *An Inconvenient Truth*, to more than 1 million people.

Carey's Tip

I work with programs to protect wildlife in forty-eight states and territories. I love NWF's campaign "Get Outdoors, It's Yours," because it is a fantastic message for both kids and parents and can help reverse the current trend of moving American childhood indoors. Parents who grew up playing outdoors, as I did, realize we love only what we know, and protect only what we love. With electronic entertainment replacing unstructured outdoor experiences, many young people are missing out on a connection with nature.

• Get outside and discover the wonders of the natural world where you live. Go exploring in your backyard, or take a hike in a park. Amazing wildlife is right outside your front door!

• Attracting birds, butterflies, and other wildlife is a fun way to enjoy nature right where you live. Imagine creating your own garden teeming with singing birds, colorful butterflies, beautiful plants, and water sources that attract wildlife. Whether you live in the country or the city, in a house or an apartment, there are things you can do to help wildlife. Container gardens, bird feeders, even a tiny water feature can be part of a city apartment windowsill or balcony. You can also adopt a public space and make it a place for wildlife. It's easier than you think!

For more great tips on attracting wildlife and creating a National Wildlife Federation Certified Wildlife Habitat, visit www.nwf.org/gardenforwildlife.

www.nwf.org/gardenforwildlife

Polar Bear and Honey Bee Advocate

Mollie Passacantando

Age: 10
Hometown:
Alexandria, Virginia

MEET MOLLIE AND HER CAUSE

My name is Mollie Passacantando. I am ten years old, and I live in Virginia. I might seem young to be an award-winning environmentalist, but believe it or not, I was actually eight when I first understood the threat that global warming posed for our planet. One day I was just your average third-grader playing tetherball on a playground, and then, suddenly, I was an animal activist addressing a crowd on Capitol Hill. And people were listening to what I have to say!

I learned about how global warming was melting all the sea ice in the Arctic when I read an article in *Time for Kids*, a magazine at school. If the ice caps were melting, polar bears could go extinct in a couple of years. It was outrageous to think that I could very well witness the extinction of this species in my lifetime. Several of my classmates read the same article, and we shared our concerns for the future of the polar bear. We had to do something to get the word out about the crisis.

RALLYING TO SAVE THE POLAR BEARS

My friends and I didn't want the polar bears to die, so we cut out some pictures of polar bears, put them on a few signs, and pasted them to our rulers. We walked around the playground at recess and told people about global warming and the polar bears and some things that they could do to help, like recycling and turning off the lights. A boy came up and said, "You can march around the playground all you want, but you're not going to do anything." My friends and I stopped our protest, realizing that we weren't helping many polar bears walking around at recess at an elementary school. That evening, I talked to my parents about how powerless I felt and how I wanted to make a difference.

BLOGGING FOR THE BEARS

My parents helped me come up with some ideas of what I could do to help the cause of the polar bears. My dad suggested I get the word out to as many people as I could. So he helped me create a blog—savethearctic .blogspot.com—with facts, photos, and directions on how to write to the U.S. Fish and Wildlife Service to support efforts to list the polar bear as an endangered species. It was a big goal, but I was very serious about making it happen. If we increase awareness about polar bears by putting them on the endangered species list, then maybe along with saving the polar bears, we can increase awareness of global warming.

Soon, I had more than a hundred kids signed up on my blog! Letters started pouring in supporting our campaign. It was hard to keep up with everything happening on the blog! My family helped, getting the word out and making sure all the letters were printed on recycled paper. Rather than forwarding e-mails, and not knowing whether anyone would ever read them, it's far more impressive and rewarding to hold a huge stack of personal letters of protest you've collected. I always wrote a thank-you note to anyone who subscribed to my blog or wrote me a letter because it's important to let people know you appreciate their attention and support.

www.savethearctic.blogspot.com

MISS MOLLIE GOES TO WASHINGTON

When I collected two hundred letters, I made arrangements with my parents' help to hand-deliver them to the U.S. Fish and Wildlife Service offices in Washington, D.C. My blog was beginning to get a lot of attention. Environmental groups were impressed that I was only eight years old yet I had such a passion and devotion to such an important cause. My story made the local news, and my Web site got tons of hits. As I was making plans to visit Washington, D.C., to deliver the letters I collected, I was invited to make a speech at Climate Crisis Day 2007 by the organizers of the event.

This event was going to be Washington's largest demonstration ever on global warming. I would be giving my speech the day before former Vice President Al Gore would be making a presentation to Congress on the need for legislative action on global warming. The rally was organized and would be attended by people who care about the Arctic. When I got to the stage that morning, I saw crowds of people wearing T-shirts, hats, and sweatshirts bearing images of polar bears, and some folks actually dressed up in polar bear costumes! I spoke to a gathering of more than a thousand people who felt the same way I did. We all wanted the U.S. Fish and Wildlife Service to list polar bears as officially threatened because, as global warming continued, there would be less and less sea ice for them to live and hunt on.

I was by far the youngest person at the rally on the steps of the Capitol that day. I was pretty nervous, but that disappeared when I began to read my speech explaining my campaign. I showed the letters I had collected to the crowd, and they cheered. We delivered the letters to the reception desk of the U.S. Fish and Wildlife Service, and I spent the rest of the day being interviewed by the media. And I never got tired because I never ran out of things to say about the cause of the polar bears.

Soon after the rally, Action for Nature (AFN), a nonprofit group that inspires young people to take action for the environment and protect the natural world in their own neighborhood and around the world, contacted me. They were impressed by all that I was doing and asked me to apply for their Young Eco Heroes Award, which recognizes young people who have taken the initiative to do something for the environment. And I was very honored when I won the award! I think it helps inspire kids around me to believe that we can change the world. But what was really more rewarding was to find out in May 2008 that the Department of the Interior designated the polar bear as threatened with extinction because of shrinking sea ice. This means that the polar bear is officially the first creature added to the endangered species list as a result of the effects of global warming. That decision is important because the government *must* help the bears by creating new laws to protect them. It also forces the government to start working on solutions for global warming. Now, that's progress!

BEES ARE THE NEXT BIG THING FOR MOLLIE

While I'm still passionate about the plight of the polar bear, nowadays, if you visit my blog, you'll notice that I'm also concerned about a different species facing potential extinction—honeybees. They're disappearing at alarming rates, and while there are many theories as to why this is happening, no one knows for sure. Bees are responsible for pollinating the plants that produce fruits and vegetables. If they disappear, so will our fresh produce. I can't find any way to put honeybees on the endangered species list, since the list doesn't focus on insects. Instead, I am talking my parents into starting a honeybee hive in our backyard. If you have any insight on the bee crisis, please contact me at savethearctic.blogspot.com!

 Mollie's TIP

If someone tells you that you're too young to make a difference, or that you can't do anything to help the planet, prove them wrong. I did. I'm still working to help polar bears and bees and any other creatures that need support. Think about how we are all connected to the animals on our planet. If they are endangered, so are we.

This Beach Is Not Your Ashtray

Chelsea Rivera

Age: 15
Hometown:
Wailuku, Hawaii

MEET CHELSEA AND HER CAUSE

My name is Chelsea Rivera. I'm fifteen, and I live in Wailuku, Hawaii. Tourists come from all over the world to visit the beautiful Hawaiian Islands, but often they don't respect that this is more than a pretty vacation spot. This special place has some amazing beaches that are also home to many marine species. Our beaches need to be clean and pristine so that they don't negatively affect the habitat of fish and other ocean wildlife. But irresponsible smokers are a huge problem, and some days the beach gets so littered that you can find more cigarette butts than shells. The thought of how this garbage might be affecting Hawaii's bountiful marine animals really upset me, and I just had to do something about it.

MARINE ANIMALS DON'T SMOKE

Some people are under the impression that cigarette butts are biodegradable, but that's not true. Cigarette butts are made of long-lasting materials, including cellulose acetate, a form of plastic, which can take up to twenty-five years to decompose. And a single butt can contain more than 165 chemicals, such as cadmium, lead, and arsenic, which can leach into the marine

environment within an hour of contact with water. Cigarette butts can poison wildlife when accidentally ingested, blocking the digestive tract or filling the stomach, resulting in malnutrition or starvation.

Cigarette butts are the most common form of marine debris, with more than 4.5 *trillion* butts littered worldwide every year. In Hawaii, one in every five items collected during coastal cleanups is a cigarette butt. So not only is smoking bad for humans, but the residue it leaves behind can kill aquatic life. I don't want people treating my home and the ocean like one big ashtray.

DOING IT ALL FOR THE WHALES

www.pacificwhale.org

I went to my dad to talk about the growing problem of our polluted beaches. My father organizes whale-

watching tours at the Pacific Whale Foundation (PWF) in Wailuku, a Maui-based nonprofit organization dedicated to promoting appreciation, understanding, and protection of whales, dolphins, coral reefs, and the ocean. I became inspired by the work that PWF does on behalf of all the inhabitants on our islands, both on land and in the sea. PWF spends a lot of time educating the

Honor Moshay

14, Eco-Equestrian, West Hollywood, California

Being a green girl to me means spending time in the outdoors with animals. Since I was a little kid, my passion has been caring for and riding horses. Some of the most fun I can have is just wandering about on my horse in the grass and trails and being a part of nature. My horse, Artie, brings me closer to the natural world; as we walk about we see birds and squirrels, and sometimes even deer, coyote, or bobcats.

Horses live in a pasture or a stall and eat a basic diet of hay (timothy grass, oats, or alfalfa) with some supplemental grain. Because horses have very delicate digestive systems, everything they eat should be pesticide- and chemical-free. For treats, I feed my horse organic carrots and apples. Instead of buying special treats, it is really simple to make your own! All you have to do is collect and chop some carrots, apples, and oats and add molasses. Mix it all together and then mush it into little balls. You can even add a little brown sugar if you want.

Horses need a lot of care. One of the things we do to care for them in southern California, where it's quite hot, is use fly and bug spray. But fly spray can have a lot of chemicals in it, so it's a good idea to use your own homemade spray and not release more toxins into the atmosphere. The U.S. Forest Service recommends an alternative, eco-friendly formula: mix 1 cup water, 1 cup Avon Skin So Soft Bath Oil, 2 cups vinegar, 1 tablespoon eucalyptus oil (found in health food stores), and an optional few tablespoons of citronella oil. Once you have combined all the ingredients, put the mixture in a spray bottle and shake well before use.

Honor's Tip

One of the great by-products of horses is that you can use their manure as garden fertilizer, and my mom says it's particularly good for roses and vegetables.

public, because while our local economy is dependent upon tourism, our unique environment is threatened by the behavior of these visitors. I felt compelled to help them and became a regular volunteer. Nothing is more satisfying for me than working side by side with my dad, coworkers, and friends. PWF is now my second home!

One of the most effective conservation campaigns at the PWF is Butts Off the Beach, which prevents littering by giving smokers no excuses. We provide smokers with brightly labeled film canisters filled with sand that they can use as temporary ashtrays. The film canisters are donated by individuals and by drugstores where film is developed. They are lightweight, convenient, and easy to use. Smokers just have to put out their cigarettes in a canister and then pocket it until they are able to dispose of the butts properly.

WHAT'S ON THE HORIZON FOR CHELSEA?

One of my jobs at the PWF is labeling the canisters and handing them out at our information stations. The canisters are available all over the state now. I also joined the beach cleanup crews, and three times a week we go to various beaches to clean up trash. I've already picked up hundreds of cigarette butts!

Chelsea's TIP

Through my volunteer work with PWF, I can see that the beaches are getting cleaner. But we still have much work ahead. It's important to respect the Earth and all its creatures. Efforts to conserve and clean up the environment won't go unnoticed.

FACT: Did you know that livestock production alone contributes 18 percent of the global warming effect? That's more than the emissions from every single car, train, and plane on the planet!

For actress and activist Alicia Silverstone, going green means eating green.

Alicia Silverstone

ALICIA'S TIP

I wasn't always a vegetarian, but I've always loved animals. If you ever get the chance to meet a cow, pig, turkey, or goat, you will see that they are just like your dog or cat—cute and funny. Like us, they want to live freely, feel love, and avoid pain. Now when I see a steak, it makes me feel sad and sick, because right away, I see my dog or the amazing cows I met at a farm sanctuary. I've been vegan for ten years, and it's the single most important decision I have ever made.

Being vegan truly is the secret to my life's joy and peace. I feel physically and spiritually better than I could have ever imagined knowing that I am doing everything I can to reduce animal suffering with simple lifestyle choices like being vegan, never purchasing any products made from animals (like wool and leather), and buying only from companies that NEVER test their products or ingredients on animals. And the bonus to my personal lifestyle choice is that by helping curb the need to produce meat, I'm helping to cut down on the significant pollution created by the process. The whole business of raising animals for food contributes significantly to global warming and the destruction of the rain forest, and dumps toxic waste into our soil and waterways—not to mention how toxic it is for you!

My tip to you is to try phasing meat out of your diet completely. There are many tasty nonanimal protein options such as beans, nuts, and yummy plant-based protein alternatives, like veggie dogs, veggie burgers, hummus, and bean stews. Talk to your parents about your interest in going "veggie." You can start out with a "Meatless Monday" and then, if you want, add on Meatless Tuesday, Wednesday, Thursday, Friday, and move through the weekend "meatless-ly." Of course, you want to make sure to eat tons of veggies and other healthy food—it's not an excuse to scarf down potato chips and sweets all day!

Go check out www.petakids.com for more info on how to balance your plate with action-packed, nutrient-rich food. Take a night to prepare one or more of the recipes on the Web site with your friends and family and share with them just how yummy meat-free meals can be!

CHAPTER 3

THE EDUCATORS
AND ARTISTS

Rain-Forest Preservationist and Climate Champion

Rebecca Chan

Reduce
Reuse
(Recycle)

Age: 17
Hometown:
Encinitas, California

MEET REBECCA AND HER CAUSE

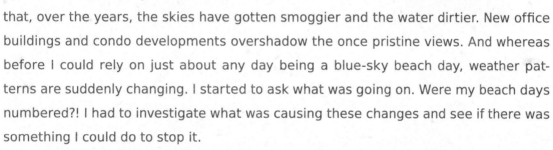

My name is Rebecca Chan. I am seventeen years old, and I'm from Encinitas, California. I grew up on the beaches of southern California and love nothing more than to soak up the sun and beauty of our coastline. But I've noticed that, over the years, the skies have gotten smoggier and the water dirtier. New office buildings and condo developments overshadow the once pristine views. And whereas before I could rely on just about any day being a blue-sky beach day, weather patterns are suddenly changing. I started to ask what was going on. Were my beach days numbered?! I had to investigate what was causing these changes and see if there was something I could do to stop it.

In ninth grade, my science teacher explained to us that our climate was changing. Climate change represents long-term and unnatural changes in the Earth's weather patterns. When the temperatures rapidly change from day to day or from year to year, it throws all of nature off balance. Air and water pollution, deforestation, and the depletion of the ozone layer are all contributors to the overall problem of climate change. And we are already seeing its effects with droughts, flooding, and the change in frequency and strength of hurricanes. I was scared after I heard this, and knew these problems were

going to get worse if we didn't do something to change it. That's what launched me into taking personal action on behalf of our planet.

I knew I had to get the word out. This was an important topic, and people needed to know about it. I wanted to educate and inspire others to take action against climate change, so I prepared a presentation based on scientific research I learned in class and on the Web. Before trying to teach about the Earth and climate change, knowing to whom you're talking is important. I find it helpful to talk first to the teachers of the classes I'll be speaking to as a way to gauge how much the audience may already know about the subject. I want to keep them engaged and inspire them to take action. Students are generally very receptive to presentations, especially when the presenters are in high school or college, people they can look up to but still relate to. The people whom I can inspire to truly care will take the extra time and effort to live more environmentally conscious lives. I try to influence as many people, preferably those my own age, as possible. When teaching about climate change, I think it's important to emphasize solutions to the various problems. I show them how they can take action by making small changes in their day-to-day lives, like using less hot water, recycling, and carpooling with their friends to school. Every little thing counts!

REBECCA SAVES THE RAIN FOREST!

Rain forests play an important part in maintaining the balance of the Earth. In 1950, about 15 percent of the Earth's surface was covered by rain forests, but today, more than half has been destroyed by illegal logging and burning. More than 200,000 acres of rain forest are burned every day, which means that more than 150 acres are lost every minute, and 78 million acres are lost every year. Burning contributes to climate change by releasing carbon dioxide into the

Simone Crew

Green Poet, Youth Speaks

I'm Simone Crew. I'm seventeen years old, and I live in San Francisco. I was inspired to write my poem "Yasmeena" because I believe that story-telling and poetry are effective ways to engage our generation in environmental issues. I was also very touched by the real Yasmeena, the girl I babysit, who helped me to understand that the environmental crisis is not a hypothetical issue, but one that is current and highly relevant even to the youngest members of our community. I hope my poem can help make the issue of global warming more relatable, and show people that it is everyone's job to care for the Earth.

I am actively involved in the organization Youth Speaks, the leading nonprofit presenter of spoken-word performance, education, and youth development programs in the country. If you want to share your green thoughts, visit www.youthspeaks.org.

Yasmeena

It really is quite sad you know, Simooone.
    People really truly should recycle more . . .

I am no one's mother,
but Yasmeena's eyes are caffeinated: lively
    and addictive.
It does not take a mother,
her hands don't fit perfectly into mine but
    we cry syncopated teardrops
our jawbones won't match up but she
    could change the world if there is still
    one for her to fix.

You don't have to be
the revolution.
Glaciers break your back if you try to carry
    them alone. Just find a Yasmeena; and
    recycle in anticipation of her breathing.

I babysit.
I have never been a revolution
neither have I made one.
I know not of being a Mother Earth, moun-
    tains never born unto my back
but like sinking topography Yasmeena's
    face slides
into a pout when bedtime arrives. And
    when she has fallen asleep I fold up the
    pizza box,
searching under the sink for the recycling
    bin,
I am not the revolution,
    but I'll heave my share of the glacier
    for Yasmeena to feel the cold.

—excerpted from the poem "Yasmeena"
by Simone G. Crew

Paulette Cole

**CEO and
Creative Director,
ABC Home**

Paulette Cole and
her daughter, Lena

While Simone uses poetic words to express her concerns about the planet and inspire others to take action, Paulette Cole spreads her eco-consciousness by greening home environments.

Paulette Cole is the CEO and creative director of ABC Home, a mission-driven platform inspiring home design as a key form of self-expression. ABC represents a new paradigm in retail, manifesting a universal exchange where spirit, sustainability, culture, currency, and creativity coexist to inform and inspire participation.

For Paulette, going green started with personal health and pregnancy. She was alarmed by the toxic chemicals put into food, cosmetics, body products, and household cleansers. As she became more conscious about buying chemical-free products for her self and her home, she realized that the Earth was ingesting these same toxins. Mother Earth became a mirror, and a profound metaphor for personal and collective well-being.

Paulette's Tip:

Consume consciously. As an antidote to empty consumerism, you can embrace your power to use your dollars, values, and individual self-expression as a way of voting to create the new green economy for a healthy planet and people.

Your personal space is a reflection of who you are and what you value—think about where your materials are coming from. You and your family can choose good wood furniture that is sourced from responsibly managed forests or that protects old growth and endangered forest species, or you can participate in a program that plants a tree for each piece of furniture you buy. Choosing vintage or antique pieces that have lasted over time is a creative way to recycle.

Visit www.abchome.com for more ideas.

www.abchome.com

atmosphere. I learned that the rain forests are essential to our survival because they turn toxic carbon dioxide into the oxygen we breathe. Also, more than half of the world's estimated 10 million species of plants, animals, and insects live in the tropical rain forest. When we cut down the forest, we leave these species with nowhere to live, leading to their possible extinction. When I heard these alarming facts, my heart sank. I could not stop thinking about all the species of plants and animals we could lose and how the rest of the world would be affected. Rain forests are in even more immediate danger than my local beaches. What started out as a concern for my beach became a passion for conserving the rain forest from further destruction by humans.

I knew I had to do something to help, so I joined and became the copresident of the rain-forest conservation club that my chemistry teacher started at my school. We are a local chapter of O_2 for Life, which is an amazing nonprofit organization dedicated to preserving the Costa Rican rain forest. The foundation protects more than five hundred acres of land located in the Osa region of Costa Rica, one of the most biodiverse areas of the world. Our club works to help conserve the rain forest by educating students in local schools through presentations about these regions. And each year we organize a variety of fund-raisers. You can take action and start a club at your school, too!

My chemistry teacher wanted our rain-forest conservation club to witness the O_2 for Life Rainforest Foundation reserve firsthand. It is located between two national parks in Costa Rica—Corcovado and Piedras Blancas. There was a lot of planning and fund-raising before our two-week summer trip, but it was all worth it—I can honestly say this trip changed my life forever. The rain forest was the most beautiful and peaceful place on Earth.

Our trip was filled with activities such as hiking

and studying the different species of plants and animals, many of which I had never seen before. But it was powerful and sad to see the areas of the forest that have been cut down.

NEXT STOP—CLIMATE CHAMPION

My trip to Costa Rica showed me that my participation in trying to help the Earth was important. I continued to hold fund-raisers for the rain forest, run our rain-forest conservation club, and give presentations to elementary- and middle-school children on the effects of climate change and rain-forest conservation. But I wanted to do more.

At the beginning of twelfth grade, I decided to tackle climate change and the deforestation of the rain forest on a global level. I wanted to show world leaders and politicians that kids do care and that we need their help to protect the environment. Through school and with the help of my mentor and chemistry teacher, I applied to be a California Climate Champion. This program is sponsored by the California Air Resources Board and the British Council. The champions in the program help with local, national, and international projects, as well as work with the media to communicate the urgency of climate change while encouraging others to make a difference. I was thrilled to learn that I was selected as one of the fifteen Climate Champions, and was then chosen to be one of the three California Climate Champions representing the United States as an International Climate Champion. The British Council's International Climate Champions (ICC) project gives teens from all over the world the opportunity to work together to combat climate change.

The International Climate Champions' first stop was London, England, where we had the task of preparing one vision statement and three specific goals to combat the issue of climate change. We were completing these to present them in person to the environmental ministers from all over the world at the 2008 G8 Summit in Kobe, Japan. The G8 Summit is an international organization where representatives from eight countries meet once a year to create solutions to global issues. The focus of this summit was the environment. Telling the ministers what kids across the world hope to do to combat climate change is a once-in-a-lifetime experience. I hoped our voices would make an impact.

Two months later, the International Climate Champions presented our ideas to the G8 Summit in Japan. I was nervous but felt strongly about our cause and was determined to get our message out there. I spoke passionately about our country's lack

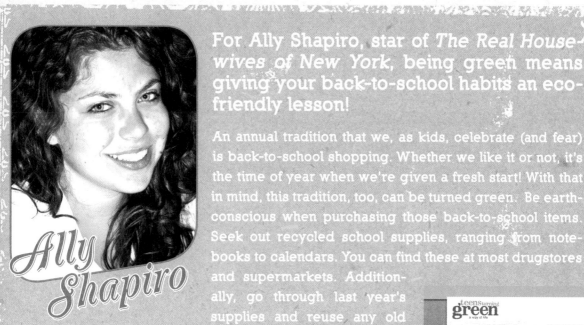

Ally Shapiro

For Ally Shapiro, star of *The Real Housewives of New York*, being green means giving your back-to-school habits an eco-friendly lesson!

An annual tradition that we, as kids, celebrate (and fear) is back-to-school shopping. Whether we like it or not, it's the time of year when we're given a fresh start! With that in mind, this tradition, too, can be turned green. Be earth-conscious when purchasing those back-to-school items. Seek out recycled school supplies, ranging from notebooks to calendars. You can find these at most drugstores and supermarkets. Additionally, go through last year's supplies and reuse any old folders, notebooks, and extra pieces of paper!

Also, talk to your teachers and administrators about getting rid of the pink soap, Purell dispensers, and eco-unfriendly dry erase-board markers in your schools. Find greener alternatives on the Web or at your nearest enviro-friendly grocery store. Benedetta Sassy Sacred Soap and Organic Rosemary and Mint Sanitizing Spray are daily must-haves from Teens Turning Green.

Find these products and more at www.teensturninggreen.org.

www.teensturninggreen.org

of commitment to combating climate change and the importance of the Kyoto Protocol. This is an international treaty aimed at controlling global warming linked to carbon dioxide and other greenhouse gases. Speaking to environmental leaders from all over the world about combating climate change was the most amazing experience I have ever had. I felt heard, and I knew I was making a difference.

WHAT'S NEXT FOR REBECCA?

Looking back on the last few years, I've learned that we can all make lasting impacts in the fight against climate change. You can never think too big! The most important thing we can do is educate ourselves on the issues. Always remember, when you are educated, you are powerful!

Rebecca's TIP

Hold a fund-raiser to collect donations for your favorite organization. My rain-forest conservation club hosts garage sales and lots of other fund-raisers, like creating screen-print T-shirts with unique and fun designs supporting our cause and selling them to teams, bands, and other schools. Remember that, when doing fund-raisers, it helps to raise awareness first, then ask for donations. People are more likely to help if they understand the issues.

Lisa Day
Associate Director, Energy Initiative, Fox Filmed Entertainment

Greening the Hollywood Scene

Like Rebecca, Lisa Day thinks big when it comes to educating the public on climate change and is using the silver screen to turn the world green.

For the first decade of her career following law school, Lisa Day was the Global Projects Director for the Earth Communications Office (ECO), a nonprofit environmental group working on climate issues. In 2006, she worked as a line producer for the feature documentary *The Eleventh Hour*, with Leonardo DiCaprio. After completing the film, Lisa spent two years as VP of Corporate and Community Affairs at Participant Productions, where she helped create and manage social action campaigns for *An Inconvenient Truth, Syriana, Good Night and Good Luck, Murderball,* and *North Country,* among others. Lisa is currently managing the Cool Change Initiative for 20th Century Fox, taking the studio carbon neutral by 2010. In addition to environmental and energy initiatives on the lot and in all international offices of Fox Filmed Entertainment, she is responsible for greening the production of all of Fox's feature films. A thoroughly green girl from her vegetarian lifestyle all the way down to her hemp shoes, Lisa has always been interested in mixing media with environmental issues and in particular, climate change, sustainable design and agriculture, alternative energy, and green transportation.

What's your carbon footprint?

All of us, no matter where we live or what we do, generate the greenhouse gases that are causing climate change. Turning on the TV, taking a shower, driving a car, eating a burger—almost everything we do has an impact. By measuring your carbon footprint—the amount of carbon dioxide your actions add to the atmosphere—you'll learn just how much of an impact your actions have. More importantly, your footprint will help you figure out what actions you can take to reduce your footprint the most. There are dozens of carbon calculators online these days, but some of my favorites are from the Nature Conservancy (www.nature.org/initiatives/climate-change/calculator) and ClimateCrisis.net (www.climatecrisis.net/takeaction/carboncalculator). You can also look at your overall environmental footprint—calculating not just carbon but the natural resources you consume and the waste you generate—by taking the Ecological Footprint quiz at www.myfootprint.org. No matter which calculator you use, don't forget to use what you've learned to take action. There are many things each of us, as individuals, can do to help stop climate change and make the world a healthier, safer place for everyone.

Devyn Howard

Global Green Cheerleader

Meet Devyn and Her Cause

I'm Devyn Howard. I'm sixteen, and I live in San Diego, California. I am a varsity cheerleader at my high school. I love being able to support the sports teams at my school and inspire a crowd with team spirit. So when I saw the film *The Eleventh Hour*, a documentary about the state of our Earth, and learned how our planet was being

threatened by global warming, I put those same cheerleading skills to work to inspire others to save our environment. Supporting organizations that are working on solutions to this problem has become my personal passion project. So I guess you can think of me as a green cheerleader, too!

One of the ways I bring my green spirit to my school, home, and neighborhood is by delivering energy-efficient compact fluorescent lightbulbs to my neighbors. This raises awareness, and also allows me to talk about the environmental charity

I'm involved in—Global Green USA. Global Green is the American arm of Green Cross International (GCI), which was created by former USSR president Mikhail S. Gorbachev. In the United States, Global Green focuses on creating green buildings and cities and educating the general public. I want to encourage other teens to come up with green actions that fit their personalities. I love talking to people about the environment. When I take energy-efficient bulbs to my neighbors, I explain the benefits of using these bulbs and show that it is convenient and easy for them to make a positive change toward a greener lifestyle. I also tell them about the organization and give them some literature about Global Green. Although it isn't much, every person who answers the door gets to learn a little about an effortless thing they can do to be more Earth-friendly. Really, how hard is it to change a lightbulb?

www.globalgreen.org

A Green Future

I believe that being green is going to be a big part of my future. I'm just looking for a bigger platform and working to develop the skills set to be the best green cheerleader I can be.

A green movement is before us, and it is young people who will be the ones to create the cleaner, safer, and healthier world for our future generations. Believing that you can be a voice that will be heard is the first step toward change. Make a point to educate others and promote the lifestyle that will preserve our planet. Go Earth! GO GREEN!

Like Devyn, Debbie Levin Uses the Spotlight to Send a Green Message

Debbie Levin, President of Environmental Media Association (EMA), has always been environmentally conscious. She began running the EMA after learning about the group's mission to utilize celebrities as green-living role models. Under Debbie's leadership, EMA has emerged as the leading entertainment organization to mobilize the entertainment industry by educating people about environmental issues, which in turn inspires them to take action. From Hollywood royalty to the hottest new celebrities to cutting-edge businesses that work toward environmental change every day, EMA is a commanding force that brings powerful people together on the path to a healthier planet. You can learn more about EMA at www.ema-online.org.

Debbie's Tip

Answer the call! If you're reluctant to trash your old cell phone because of its toxic components, there's something else you can do. Did you know that you can recycle old cell phones? Log on to www.ema-online.org to find out more. You can also donate your cell phone. Go online to find out how!

www.ema-online.org

77

Changing the World, One Quilted Square at a Time

Casey Ehrlich

Age: 16
Hometown:
Marblehead,
Massachusetts

MEET CASEY AND HER CAUSE

I'm Casey Ehrlich, and I'm sixteen years old. I live in Marblehead, Massachusetts, and enjoy music, art, skiing in New Hampshire, and hanging out with my family and our two dogs. I come from a very politically active family. My mom has been involved in environmental issues, public policy, and politics for my entire life, and I think it's rubbing off on me.

While watching the news on Earth Day in 2007, my mom, little sister, and I started talking about how sad it was that animal species were vanishing and pollution was getting worse. Every day news reports update us on pressing environmental issues plaguing our planet, such as global warming, toxic waste, and air pollution. It can feel hopeless, especially if you can't vote.

Despite having grown up in a family involved in local politics, even I sometimes felt completely powerless and afraid. If I felt this way, I was guessing that other kids, especially those younger than me, must be really frightened about the future of life on our planet. I did more research after Earth Day, and the more I read about global warming and other environmental issues, the more I felt I had to do something.

CASEY TURNS HELPLESS INTO HOPEFUL

I thought it would be great for kids to be able to express their feelings of "eco-anxiety" through an art project. I thought about different ways to display this, and I came up with the idea of asking kids to design and decorate squares of recycled clothing or fabric. I'd put all the squares together to make a quilt. My mom and sister volunteered to help me, even though none of us had ever sewn anything before. And we started with squares of our own!

CASEY STARTS BLANKET THE GLOBE!

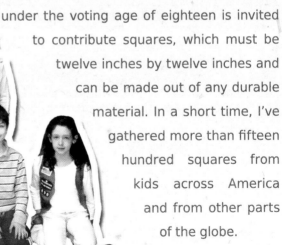

A day later we decided to post our project on the Web and created the site www.blankettheglobe.com, where we asked other kids to contribute squares to our quilt. I then needed to get the word out, so I approached two local Girl Scout troops and asked the children I student teach at my local synagogue. My sister asked her fifth-grade class, and I spoke to my high school principal, who connected me with the textile class. Just through word of mouth, the news of my cause began to spread. And I was soon working with larger organizations in Boston.

Then, thanks to the global reach of the Web site, squares began arriving from all over the world. My art project was giving people a voice. It was amazing! Anyone under the voting age of eighteen is invited to contribute squares, which must be twelve inches by twelve inches and can be made out of any durable material. In a short time, I've gathered more than fifteen hundred squares from kids across America and from other parts of the globe.

CASEY'S QUILT CONNECTS KIDS TO NATURE

As my organization grew, we adopted the following mission statement: "To build awareness, give voice to the environmental concerns of children, and, through creative expression, empower them to participate in protecting the Earth's natural resources for their future." So many people ask what I'm going to do with the quilt when it's done, but if you consider the mission of giving a voice to children, I always hold open the possibility that the project may never end. But still, along the way, I plan on making as big of a deal as I can with the stunning visual impact of the combination of all of the children's beautiful artwork. The bigger the piece gets, the louder our voices will be heard.

And our cause has gone viral on the Web, with both local and international press mentioning the Web site and bringing in lots of interest from kids all over the planet to contribute squares. I frequently speak at schools and community centers and give interviews to the media encouraging other children to design squares for the quilt. To help them get started on their square, I suggest that they illustrate how they feel they are most connected to nature. Some choose an endangered species, while others illustrate the importance of recycling and using renewable energy. Their messages are usually

very positive. I think that this particular part of the project is the most important: often I see the kids looking up at the sky or looking around them for inspiration, and at that moment I know they are thinking about themselves in nature. Because of that moment, I hope they take recycling and conservation seriously. Once you feel connected, you realize that any carelessness ripples through nature and affects us all.

Even though it looks easy, I do spend a lot of time on this project getting all the squares together, visiting with kids, and ensuring that all the kids can find their squares on the Web site. It is extremely rewarding to know that I have made so many kids aware of the environmental crisis and have given them a sense of empowerment. Each square represents one child committed to helping the planet, and I like to imagine all the children, with all their squares, adding up to a big green army, a powerful force for positive change.

THE QUILT SPREADS THE WARNING ABOUT GLOBAL WARMING

With all the squares from around the globe, my quilt is getting huge, which tells me that my idea to generate awareness is working. But the best way to measure how much the project has accomplished is through feedback. I often get e-mails from kids who find the Web site and have questions or comments. Most inquiries are from kids asking me to bring it to their schools or groups, and even requests to tour the quilt to other countries.

The kids and adults I've met through this work give me so much hope for the future that I didn't have when I started this project. I'd like to continue sharing that spirit with all kids who may not know that there are so many people who care. To that end, I have created a program called the Blanket the Globe Ambassadors in which anyone who is responsible for collecting fifty or more squares gets a Blanket the Globe canvas bag as a prize. The great things about this prize are that it publicizes the project and it cuts down on the use of plastic bags!

WHAT'S NEXT FOR CASEY?

There are three things this project still needs—people willing to sew panels, fabric donations, and, most important, people out there spreading the word about the project. My goal is to continue gathering and sewing squares onto the quilt until it fills a football stadium. Then I would like to travel to Washington, D.C., with it and let the adults who make our public policies know that they need to do all they can to protect the world for the next generations.

Casey's TIP

If you are a younger teen, there are plenty of things you can do to conserve energy and help the environment. Unplug your electronics and chargers when you're not using them. That means your cell phone charger, too! Even though they're not turned on or there's nothing attached, they are still drawing electricity. The estimated electrical load drained from appliances and electronics in standby mode accounts for 18 million tons of CO_2 emissions each year. (Plus, you'll get points from your parents for helping save on the electric bill!)

Zem Joaquin

Green Style Expert

Zem Joaquin has always been a green girl. Today, she's a green style expert, green design and strategy consultant, and founder of the blog www.ecofabulous.com. She's also a board member and San Francisco chair of Global Green USA, a board member of Healthy Child Healthy World, and a founding member of the Cradle-to-Cradle Conference.

Cradle-to-Cradle is a philosophy that means that everything we create should either biodegrade and eventually be absorbed back into the soil or should have a plan for reuse. That way, nothing ends up in a landfill. All products should be healthy for the people who make them, for the people who use them, and for the environment.

Ask the Right Questions When Shopping for Clothes and Shoes!

ZEM'S SHOPPING CHECKLIST

WHAT IS THE ITEM MADE OF?

It is very important to choose nontoxic fabrics, both for the health of our bodies and for the Earth. The best choices are fabrics made of recycled material and organic fabrics made from rapidly renewable resources. Here are a few materials I like.

ORGANIC COTTON: Did you know that a third of a pound of pesticides is used in the production of enough traditional cotton to make a single cotton T-shirt, and two-thirds of a pound for a pair of jeans? Pesticides and toxins are really bad for us, for the soil we grow food in, for the water we drink, and for the air we breathe. So always try to choose organic cotton!

RECYCLED PET or RECYCLED POLYESTER: It's so much better to use these recycled synthetic materials than to create entirely new things. It cuts down on pollution and energy waste.

BAMBOO and HEMP: These are great fibers to use because the plants are rapidly renewable resources; that is, both plants grow very quickly.

100% POLYESTE

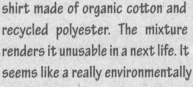

TENCEL: This wood pulp is reformulated to make natural fibers that are strong and durable.

MODAL: This fiber is made from beech trees and is similar to cotton or rayon.

WHAT WILL HAPPEN TO YOUR CLOTHES AFTER YOU ARE FINISHED WITH THEM?

Each American throws away an average of sixty-eight pounds of clothing and textiles annually, and this figure is increasing every year, so we all need to do our part! When you're finished using these clothes, you should donate them to a local charity so others can enjoy them. But if they are worn out, there are some companies that take back old clothing and accessories to turn them into new clothes.

WHERE IS IT MADE?

Try to find things that are made as close to home as possible. If you live in St. Louis and are buying a T-shirt that was made overseas, a lot of fuel was wasted just to get your T-shirt to you! If you choose clothes that were made in your country, you are also supporting your country's economy by helping more people keep their jobs. Finally, in some underdeveloped countries, unfair labor practices occur in order to manufacture clothing. By buying clothes from these countries or companies, you are unknowingly supporting these bad labor conditions.

THINGS TO BE WARY OF

Clothing that is composed of both biodegradable and nonbiodegradable materials, such as a shirt made of organic cotton and recycled polyester. The mixture renders it unusable in a next life. It seems like a really environmentally friendly idea, but mixing man-made materials with natural materials makes them both unusable when the shirt gets stained or goes out of style. Pure (ideally organic) cotton, which like wool, is a natural material, will eventually just get broken down by tiny organisms and be absorbed back into the soil. Man-made fabric, like polyester, can take hundreds of years to break down, so there needs to be a plan in place for what will happen to it when it doesn't serve a purpose any longer. Pure polyester can actually be recycled back into more clothing or can become another product like carpet. But if you mix the two fabrics, the natural material will no longer break down thanks to the synthetic (man-made) yarn, and the synthetic material loses much of its strength as well, so they both become useless. Therefore, look for 100 percent organic cotton or wool or 100 percent recycled PET or polyester.

ADHESIVES WITH FORMALDEHYDE

One of the most common and dangerous toxins in the environment. These are most commonly found in shoes.

THINGS LABELED BIODEGRADABLE COTTON

This usually means that it is just traditional cotton, and these companies are trying to trick you into thinking you are making an eco-friendly choice!

For friends and eco-bloggers *Megan Kuhlmann, Rachel McAdams,* and *Didi Bethurum,* going green is much more fun when they're doing it together.

The three of us are longtime dedicated green girls who love exchanging tips on ways to reduce our impact on the environment. When we realized that exchanging eco-tips was becoming daily conversation, we decided to do something about it. In May 2007, we launched greenissexy .org, a Web site dedicated to showing the world that tiny life changes can make a big impact. Why sexy? Because being informed is sexy. Being responsible is sexy. Being eco-friendly is sexy. Making a difference is sexy. We invite you to become part of the green-is-sexy community by helping us change the world one day at a time. Greenissexy.org is a place where we can combine all our different interests, talents, resources, and experiences. Right now Didi is into geeky computer things, comedy, and Bikram yoga. Rachel likes slow walking, fast biking, passion fruit, and her cowboy boots. Megan is currently into DIY home-improvement projects and finally teaching herself to cook.

www.greenissexy.org

OUR TIP TO YOU:

Go green with your friends! Every change you make on your own helps the planet, but if you band together with other green girls, you're creating a powerful force of nature!

CHAPTER 4
THE RECYCLERS

Combating Global Warming with the 3 R's

Isabel Bush

Age: 18
Hometown:
Juneau, Alaska

MEET ISABEL AND HER CAUSE

I'm Isabel Bush from Juneau, Alaska, and I'm eighteen years old. I like to think I am pretty adventurous. You can usually find me doing outdoor activities such as mountain climbing, hiking, fishing, kayaking, and camping with my family and friends in the Alaskan wilderness. I feel so lucky to have grown up in Juneau. It is a beautiful place sandwiched between snow-covered mountains and the deep blue ocean.

A few years ago, my love of the outdoors led me to become passionate about preserving the nature in Alaska. My older sister was a member of the organization Alaska Youth for Environmental Action (AYEA) and inspired me to join. AYEA is a high school environmental education and leadership program that inspires, educates, and takes action on environmental issues facing our communities. It is the Alaska arm of the National Wildlife Federation's national high school program called Earth Tomorrow.

Through the organization, I learned that global warming is a serious problem. As chairman of the Juneau chapter, I've been able to meet kids from other AYEA chapters in Alaska, and have found out that the effects of global warming are everywhere—from small Alaskan villages to larger cities.

Rising temperatures have caused risks of flooding and erosion due to higher ocean water levels, and in many places, some of Alaska's permafrost has thawed. This is a

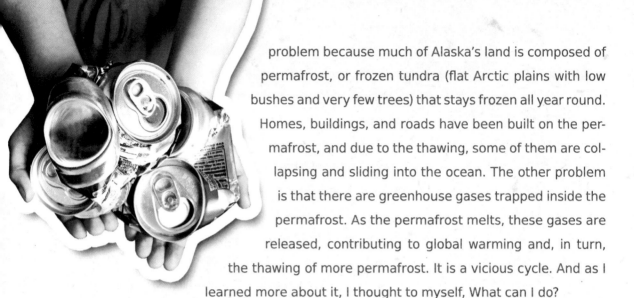

problem because much of Alaska's land is composed of permafrost, or frozen tundra (flat Arctic plains with low bushes and very few trees) that stays frozen all year round. Homes, buildings, and roads have been built on the permafrost, and due to the thawing, some of them are collapsing and sliding into the ocean. The other problem is that there are greenhouse gases trapped inside the permafrost. As the permafrost melts, these gases are released, contributing to global warming and, in turn, the thawing of more permafrost. It is a vicious cycle. And as I learned more about it, I thought to myself, What can I do?

REDUCE, REUSE, AND RECYCLE TO PREVENT GLOBAL WARMING

I did some research and learned that we can help combat global warming by reducing, reusing, and recycling (the three R's). Manufacturing, distributing, and using new products results in greenhouse gas emissions, which contribute to global warming. Increased concentrations of these gases can contribute to rising global temperatures, sea level changes, and other climate changes. According to the Environmental Protection Agency, recycling saves energy and helps prevent global warming. It is a simple concept, but it really does make a difference! When people reuse goods or when products are made with less material, less energy is needed to extract, transport, and process raw materials and to manufacture products. When energy demand decreases, fewer fossil fuels are burned and less carbon dioxide is emitted into the atmosphere.

The three R's are especially important in my community. Juneau's landfill has less than a thirty-year life capacity, which means that the landfill can hold only the amount of waste that will pile up over thirty years. And unfortunately it is filling up fast. I did more research and realized that not only was the landfill filling up with trash, it was filling up with recyclable products, too! Something had to be done!

Sibella Dowad
Green Islander

I'm Sibella Dowad. I'm twelve years old, and I spend my summers on a totally green island. Here on Bowen Island, Canada, people do everything they can to recycle. Many of the people here are second- and third-generation residents, so they have a very special connection to this place.

Surrounded by majestic hills and the Pacific Ocean, about three thousand people call this island their home. Howe Sound looks like a Norwegian fjord, and across the water in the distance are the snowcapped mountains of Whistler. People here take great pride in the surrounding landscape and have a very healthy respect for Mother Nature. But it is a small island with a finite amount of space and resources, so recycling is a huge part of our everyday lives.

There is a very big recycling drop-off on the island, where everything you can think of is separated into different categories. People bring their paper, plastics, glass, and even electronics, and they are thoroughly sorted and everything is recycled. Big plastic bottles at the market can be refilled with filtered water. Milk comes in glass bottles, and each time one is returned empty and clean, you get a dollar back!

The islanders have only one small garbage container to last for a whole week, so this encourages careful disposal of everything that comes into the house. Everyone always takes reusable baskets to shop for groceries, as plastic bags are one item the recycling plant doesn't take here! Everyone finds ways of reusing items rather than throwing them away. When you breathe the clean air and swim in the cool, clean ocean, you understand how important being environmentally conscious really is.

When I go back to Los Angeles each August, I keep up the vigilant recycling practices in my home and at school. Even though people on Bowen Island need to be extra environmentally conscious to survive, I apply that same sense of urgency to life in the big city and beyond. It's important to think of the world as just one tiny island, where every action we take has consequences.

One thing I noticed was that my town did not have a recycling program set up. I was determined to change that. Our AYEA chapter decided to take action, and our first stop would be our schools. We wanted to educate students on the effects of global warming and the importance of recycling. I needed a little guidance on how to get this started, so I joined Friends of Recycling, a local citizens' action group in Juneau. The members were very helpful and told me where to buy the bins, whom to contact about obtaining a business recycling license, and how to contact local recycling pickup companies. With this information, the wheels were set in motion.

Setting up a recycling program wasn't easy, and we ran into some roadblocks along the way. The school administration and staff were not taking us seriously, and our first few attempts to set up plastic recycling bins and the service failed. But we kept trying. We told the administration how frustrated we were, and after several months they finally listened. We were able to set up the recycling program, which includes recycling mixed paper, plastic, and aluminum. It was a true team effort—we couldn't have done this without the students and teachers who volunteered to drive the recyclables out to the recycling center. We are still working on creating a recycling program for our whole school district, and our team won't stop until it is set up!

Mischa Barton

FOR ACTRESS MISCHA BARTON, BEING GREEN IS ALL IN THE BAG.

When you go to the grocery store, use the re-usable bags that you can bring back with you to avoid using the paper and plastic versions, so long as you can remember to bring them with you. Remembering can be the tricky part, but it's much better for the environment.

Janee Becker, Linda Geiger, and Vanessa Crew

City Recycling

We are Janee Becker, Linda Geiger, and Vanessa Crew. We're each seventeen years old, and we live in Dike, Iowa. Each of us is unique, but we share a passion for helping the environment. After our county landfill closed last year, we were inspired to take action. Dike had only a once-a-month curbside-recycling program, so members of our community were less likely to make recycling part of their everyday lives. Many recyclables ended up in our landfill, causing it to fill up too fast. This is happening all over the United States, and landfills are closing at a rapid rate.

We knew we had to do something, but we needed help. We wanted to set up a recycling collection site so people would have a place to bring their recycling. We went to one of our teachers, who helped us partner with our local sanitation company. The sanitation company was supportive of the recycling collection site because they

felt this would help more people recycle. They agreed to provide the containers, pick up the recycling when the bins are full, and drop them off at the nearest recycling center about twenty miles away. We all worked together to prepare a proposal to start a drop-off recycling site in Dike, and we took our proposal to the Dike City Council. Initially, the idea of three teenagers starting a recycling collection site made them a bit hesitant, but we assured the council that we would monitor the collection site to make sure people were following the rules. After a month of deliberation, they passed our proposal!

We set up six huge recycling bins for cardboard, plastics, mixed paper, and aluminum cans. We went door-to-door and handed out recycling brochures explaining the importance of recycling, where our center was located, and what products you could recycle there. Five days after the opening, a few of the bins were already full! It was an amazing accomplishment, and we are thrilled to see how many more people are recycling in our hometown!

ISABEL INSPIRES ALL OF JUNEAU

I was very proud of our accomplishments at our school, but I knew this was only a first step. My next goal was to green up our entire town through recycling. I went back to Friends of Recycling and helped them set up monthly citywide magazine recycling drives. Once the city saw that magazines could be easily recycled and that there was interest in the community to do so, they took over and added magazines to the list of things that could be recycled at our city recycling center. Then I learned that November

15 was America Recycles Day. You can learn more about this event at www.nrc-recycle.org. I wanted to make November 15 Juneau Recycles Day, so I talked to Friends of Recycling again. They helped me draft a proclamation to send to the mayor for approval. The mayor was thrilled and officially proclaimed November 15 as Juneau Recycles Day! We used this day to educate students at our own school about what can be recycled and where it can be recycled in our town. This was an amazing achievement, and from that day forward, I knew that if I put my mind to something, there was nothing that could get in my way.

ISABEL'S GREEN FUTURE

I plan to continue educating others about the importance of recycling and the effects of global warming. I want to take care of Alaska so that future generations can enjoy everything our beautiful state has to offer. I think it is great to dream big but it is important to understand that we can make small goals for ourselves to help tackle larger problems.

Americans are reducing, reusing, and recycling to help solve the global crisis; we just need to do more of it. Every second, fifteen hundred aluminum cans are recycled in the United States. This makes a big difference! If we all work together and focus on what we can do to create positive change, we will make a lasting impact!

Isabel's TIP

BE CREATIVE WITH PLASTICS! We all know certain plastics are bad for the environment. We recycle what we can, but there are other ways to reuse plastic. Braid plastic bag strips into friendship bracelets; crochet them into rugs and hats; iron them into sturdier bags. For an AYEA community dinner, we made candleholders out of plastic bottles and streamers out of colored plastic bags. While it's best not to use any plastic, reuse what you can at all times.

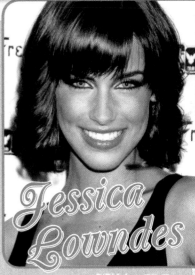

FOR JESSICA LOWNDES, STAR OF *90210*, GOING GREEN MEANS DITCHING THOSE PLASTIC BOTTLES AND TAPPING INTO YOUR HOME FAUCET!

Did you know that bottled water produces up to 1.5 million tons of plastic waste per year? Not only that, but according to Food and Water Watch, the plastic used in water bottles requires up to 47 million gallons of oil per year to produce! This means that even if you recycle your water bottles (which you should), just by buying them in the first place you are increasing your carbon footprint. My advice is to buy an inexpensive drinking water filter for your home faucet. Not only is it better for the environment, but it actually might be better for you. The Environmental Protection Agency, which oversees tap water, actually has stricter water-quality standards than the Food and Drug Administration, which oversees bottled water. For more information, visit www.foodandwaterwatch.org/water/bottled.

www.foodandwaterwatch.org/water/bottled

Zoe Fuller

Zoe Rethinks Plastics

I'm Zoe Fuller from Palmer, Alaska. I am fifteen years old, and like Isabel, I am a member of Alaska Youth for Environmental Action (AYEA). I joined the green movement after seeing several garbage dumps become blemishes on our gorgeous landscape. Some Alaskan communities don't have proper landfills, and you can tell where the garbage dump is from miles away by the plastic shopping bags blowing in the wind and littering the countryside. Plastics make up a large percentage of our waste nationwide, and they never fully decompose.

Plastic pollutes not only our land but also our oceans and waterways. Seabirds and other wildlife are washing up on shore entangled in things like plastic nets and other scraps of plastic. Daily, 60 million plastic bottles are thrown away, and many of them end up in the ocean. Did you know that in the Pacific Ocean, there is something called the Great Pacific Garbage Patch? This is 3.5 million tons of trash floating in the ocean between northern California and Hawaii. The garbage patch is twice the size of Texas and most of the trash is plastic!

Plastic products never biodegrade, they photodegrade. Biodegradation is the process whereby organic substances are broken down by enzymes produced by living organisms. Biodegradable matter is generally organic material such as plant and animal matter and other substances originating from living organisms, or artificial materials that are similar enough to plant and animal matter to be put to use by microorganisms. Photodegradation is when materials are broken down by the absorption of photons found in sunlight and other forms of light. Through photodegradation, materials break down into minuscule bits but never go away. These particles harm the fish and other wildlife that ingest them. We all contribute to the plastic problem, but the good news is we can contribute to the solution, too!

As a member of AYEA, I get to work with other teens who are as passionate as I am about preserving our Alaskan wilderness. There's strength in numbers, and with so many of us eager to help, we can really make things happen to ensure Alaska's natural beauty for generations to come. In November 2007, I attended an AYEA leaders' conference and met leaders,

including Isabel, from other AYEA chapters. We talked about which environmental issues were relevant to all Alaskan communities, and from there, we decided that our goal was "to reduce plastic waste in Alaskan communities through education and action." We decided to do a statewide campaign to create awareness, called "R3 Rethink Plastics," and I was elected chairman. The R3 stands for Reduce, Reuse, Recycle. Rethink signifies that we need to totally rethink our outlook on how we treat our Earth. First, decide what plastic products you can do without. Then, Reduce: Reduce how much you buy. For certain necessities, buy in bulk. It not only has less packaging, but it costs less, too. Reuse: Invest in cloth shopping bags, reusable containers for your lunches, and reusable water bottles. We all slip sometimes, and if you end up with a disposable water bottle, keep

refilling it. If you end up with a plastic grocery bag, use it to line your garbage can. Recycle: Make sure to have two trash bins at home clearly labeled RECYCLING and TRASH. If your community has a recycling center, you should drop off your recyclables there.

To promote the campaign, we created educational materials about the harm that plastic can pose when it is overused. We finished up the campaign in April with a Week Without Plastics, when people were encouraged to think about how they use plastic and what they could do to reduce their plastic use. During the week we

talked to people at grocery stores and encouraged them to rethink their plastic consumption. I also gave two presentations to middle-school students about plastics, did a trash pickup, and had an article I wrote about plastics published in two newspapers and one newsletter. My AYEA chapter hosted a table at an Earth Day event to educate the community about plastics. We also helped raise funds for our local recycling center. We were determined to raise awareness, and we succeeded in helping reduce plastic waste in Alaskan landfills, communities, and homes.

Abbe Hamilton

18, Girl Scouts of Central and Western Massachusetts
South Hadley, Massachusetts

Girl Scouts Go Green!

Hi, I'm Abbe. I was concerned about wastefulness at my school and its impact on the environment, and decided to do something about it!

I started a food-waste composting pilot program at my school, South Hadley High School. I worked with a science teacher, the town's solid-waste director, the state's Department of Environmental Protection, and members of the school's Environmental Club to plan and execute the project. As part of the pilot program, students use biodegradable plates and cups and place uneaten food in the compost bin. As a result of the project, my school's waste was reduced from 85 percent to 25 percent in just one school year.

Neighboring schools have contacted my school to replicate the program. I have also been sharing my knowledge with the community by speaking at the Massachusetts Agriculture in the Classroom conference and hosting teach-ins at Whole Foods Market. In October 2008, I earned a Girl Scouts' Gold Award, and was named one of the 2008 National Young Women of Distinction. This is the highest national honor awarded by the organization for extraordinary leadership and community service.

I've been a Girl Scout for thirteen years and scouting has taught me that when I discover a problem that needs to be solved, such as the current environmental crisis, I have the skills and the power to help fix it. What's really great is that with Girl Scouts, I'm never alone when taking on challenges because I have the opportunity to connect with other girls who care about the environment and want to bring about sustainable change. Girl Scouts is always there to support my efforts—as an environmentalist, as a leader, and as a girl!

Abbe's Tip

Go green by becoming a Girl Scout! Join our Girl Scout Community Action Project and help green your school. Girl Scouts all over the country are working on a signature annual community action project focused on teaming up with their schools and communities to improve air quality, energy use, water use, waste management, and the use of green space. When Girl Scouts celebrates its hundredth anniversary in 2012, we'll have two great reasons to party: our organization's

centennial and the positive impact on the environment achieved by our members. Find out more about Girl Scouts at www.girlscouts.org, and join Girl Scouts today!

About Girl Scouts

Founded in 1912, Girl Scouts of the USA is the preeminent leadership development organization for girls, with 3.4 million girls and adult members worldwide. Girl Scouts is the leading authority on girls' healthy development, and builds girls of courage, confidence, and character who make the world a better place. The organization serves girls from every corner of the United States and its territories. Girl Scouts of the USA also serves American girls and their classmates attending American or international schools overseas in ninety countries. For more information on how to join, volunteer, reconnect, or donate to Girl Scouts, call (800) GSUSA4U (800-478-7248) or visit www.girlscouts.org.

www.girlscouts.org

Mia Wasilevich's
Environista Extraordinaire

WRAP IT UP: PLASTIC SAFETY TIP

There are some plastics that are actually safer for you and the environment, some to use with caution, and others to avoid altogether. Ideally, the safe ones would be nonpetroleum-based, nonleaching, reusable, and recyclable or biodegradable (some of the new stuff coming on the market is made from corn or sugar). In a nutshell:

SAFER:
Polyethylene terephthalate (PET or PETE) (#1)
High-density polyethylene (HDPE) (#2)
Low-density polyethylene (LDPE) (#4)
Polypropylene (PP) (#5)

AVOID:
Polyvinyl chloride (PVC) (#3)
Polystyrene (#6)

USE WITH CAUTION:
Polycarbonate/Other (#7)

There is another group of chemicals, called phthalates, that are sometimes added to plastics to make them flexible and less brittle. Phthalates are environmental contaminants that can harm our bodies. If you heat up plastics (e.g., heating up your dinner in a plastic container in the microwave), you could increase the leaching of phthalates from the containers into water and food. A simple rule of thumb: transfer your food to a nonplastic glass or microwave-safe container before you heat it up.

RECYCLING 101: THE BASICS

Originally taken from the National Recycling Coalition: www.nrc-recycle.org/dos.aspx

EVERY COMMUNITY HAS ITS OWN GUIDELINES FOR WHAT SHOULD AND SHOULD NOT BE RECYCLED. CALL YOUR LOCAL PUBLIC WORKS DEPARTMENT OR RECYCLING ORGANIZATION TO FIND OUT THE DETAILS. THAT WAY YOU CAN BE SURE YOU'RE DOING YOUR PART, AND DOING IT RIGHT.

CLEANLINESS COUNTS

Rinsing cans and keeping boxes out of the weather makes them easier to process. That keeps costs down.

IF SUPPLIED WITH A BIN, PAY ATTENTION TO WHAT GOES IN

Take it upon yourself to be an accurate recycler. A cereal box is probably great, but a greasy pizza box may not be. Maybe milk jugs are good, but not the caps. Check the lid of your recycling bin for guidelines, or call or visit your municipal Web site to find out the rules.

GOOD BETS

Steel cans, aluminum cans, newspapers, magazines, catalogs, junk mail, plastic beverage bottles, milk jugs, glass bottles and jars, cereal boxes, and other clean and dry cardboard boxes are probably recyclable at your local recycling center.

PROBABLY NOT

Styrofoam, lightbulbs, food-soiled paper, wax paper, and ceramics are probably not recyclable. Be aware and try to use less of these materials.

DO RECYCLE ELECTRONICS

Recycle your old computers and cell phones. Check out Dell, Staples, and Waste Management Recycle America Web sites for information on how you can recycle these items.

HAZARDOUS WASTES HAVE THEIR PLACE

Household hazardous wastes, like paint cans, motor oil, antifreeze, car batteries, pesticides, pool chemicals, etc., usually need to be disposed of separately. Again, check your community resources and guidelines.

For more information, visit the the National Recycling Coalition at www.nrc-recycle.org.

WHAT GETS RECYCLED INTO WHAT?

Originally taken from www.nrc-recycle.org/interestingendproducts.aspx

Sometimes recyclable products are recycled into exactly what you'd expect. Old newspapers are recycled into new newspapers, and old glass bottles are recycled into new glass bottles. However, there are thousands of different products created out of recycled materials! Here are just a few.

GLASS BEVERAGE CONTAINERS are recycled into materials for roads, marbles, decorative tiles, surfboards, and jewelry.

FIVE PLASTIC SODA BOTTLES yield enough fiber for one extra-large T-shirt, one square foot of carpet, or enough fiber to fill one ski jacket.

PLASTIC BOTTLES are also recycled into carpet, park benches, picnic tables, pipes, flowerpots, and sleeping bags.

MILK JUGS are recycled into sandbox toys, tea sets, and cookware.

STEEL AND ALUMINUM CANS are recycled into new cars, bikes, appliances, cookware, lawn chairs, window frames, toys, fire hydrants, and tools.

NEWSPAPER is recycled into festive wrapping paper, construction paper, tissues, game boards, animal bedding, puzzles, and telephone books.

WORN-OUT SNEAKERS are recycled into material used in basketball courts, tennis courts, athletic fields, running tracks, and playgrounds.

TIRES are recycled into shoes, purses, raincoats, umbrellas, farm tools, and hats.

FLIP-FLOPS are recycled into doormats, jewelry, toys, and furniture.

MIXED PAPER is recycled into tissues; napkins; paper towels; school supplies such as folders, index cards, and notebooks; and even cat litter.

CARDBOARD is recycled into brown paper lunch bags, cereal boxes, and soap boxes.

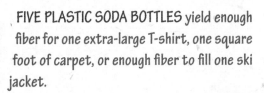

Jordan Howard
Earth-Positive Living

Meet Jordan and Her Cause

I'm Jordan. I'm sixteen, and I live in Gardena, California. Not so long ago, I was skeptical of being green, and I didn't hesitate to share my thoughts with my teachers and classmates at the Environmental Charter High School. Part of the curriculum is environmental leadership training through their program Green Ambassadors. It's an environmental-education program that empowers youth to be agents of change in their communities and world. Students were excited to learn about solar panels and recycling, but for me, the whole green movement seemed like just too much work. But everything changed in October 2006, when I was selected to go to the Bioneers Youth Conference.

At the conference, the exhibition halls were filled with alternative green products, the eco-friendly versions of household items. It was like opening a door to the future, a better "Earth-positive" world, and it opened up my mind, too. I saw so many Earth-positive solutions and met people who dedicate their lives to teaching others about being environmentally conscious. And there seemed to be a healthy green alternative for everything I use every day. On display I saw

corn-based plastic bags, corn-based cups, potato forks, and even plates made out of sugarcane—all of which biodegrade in compost in under eighty days. Trash that disappears like magic! I suddenly realized that there was no reason not to be green. It didn't really require any extra effort at all, and it makes so much sense. What really mystified me is that if these green alternatives are readily available and can actually help save the planet, why isn't everyone using them?

I came home from the conference buzzing with a green agenda. I raced through my house telling my parents everything they needed to change. Then I took them to a green market and made them load up on organic produce. We bought reusable grocery bags and swore off plastic bags that day. Then we set up a compost pile in the backyard. It was surprisingly easy to get my family to stop using the garbage disposal after meals and to throw their organic leftovers onto the pile. Pretty soon I saw my parents competing with each other over who carried more green bags in their car trunk!

A Baby Shower Goes Green

I guess it should come as no surprise to me that my parents supported my desire to make our home Earth-positive. They always want what is best for my siblings and me. And when my mom was expecting another baby, I just had to have a green shower for her! I sent out invitations printed on recycled paper, and asked my relatives to help me host an organic party. We prepared food we had purchased at the farmers market, and used corn-based cups, sugar-based plates, and virgin pulp napkins (100 percent compostable). I registered a gift list on a "green baby shower" Web site, and we asked guests to bring their gifts unwrapped or inside something that could be reused. It was fun finding creative ways to throw a green baby shower, and I realized that I could do the same for birthdays, sweet sixteen parties, and holidays. The possibilities were endless!

The green shower was a great opportunity for my relatives and friends to experience Earth-positive alternatives. They asked me a lot of questions, and I covered the basics of adopting a green lifestyle, which, for me, means using zero plastics, conserving energy, adopting solar options, and buying only green products. I had become a green ambassador, a leader in my community to educate, inspire, and bring about environmental change. Now there was no stopping me!

A Green Ambassador Spreads the Word

I needed to spread the green word on a larger scale, so I helped found Green Ambassador Productions, a filmmaking and event-production arm of our school program. I directed a film entitled *A Day in the Life*, which depicts a family of seven doing ordinary things throughout the day in two ways—Earth-negative and Earth-positive. For example, we show a girl brushing her teeth with the water running. Then the film "rewinds" and shows her brushing her teeth the green way, by turning off the water. The film is full of helpful green tips, and to date, more than seven hundred people have seen it and even more have heard about it.

I've changed as a result of joining the Green Ambassadors program, and people see and admire the leader I've become. My friends and classmates look up to me and follow my example. I feel a personal responsibility to share my Earth-positive education with others. I want to transform this world into a place that no longer needs environmentalists and environmental groups, and where being Earth-positive is a unified state of mind.

To find out more about how your school can start a Green Ambassadors program, visit www.greenambassadors.org.

Sara Laimon

Founder/Program Director of Green Ambassadors

Jordan credits her teacher and mentor, Sara Laimon, for turning her gratefully green.

Sara Laimon, founder of Green Ambassadors, is an educator at Environmental Charter High School in southern California, where she has taught and mentored the next generation of environmental leaders. Sara has been a positive light within the sustainability movement for the past ten years. She officially became a green girl when, at age seventeen, she ran for the city board with a platform for greening her hometown of Pewaukee, Wisconsin. She lost by only three votes, but this did not stop her from pursuing her passion to create change. At age twenty, she started a dairy farm in Zimbabwe, which was the green spark that led her to understand how U.S. systems needed to change in order for the rest of the world to have a sustainable model to follow.

Since that time, she has spent her life educating youth about sustainability and seeking unique and varied ways to reach this important audience. Sara teaches the importance of actively contributing and being a steward of this planet. During her career as a classroom teacher, she has guided classes and school groups to convert a diesel car to run on veggie oil, create biodiesel fuel, and eat organic. Sara has traveled to Brazil, Colombia, Argentina, Haiti, Greece, and the Galápagos finding, sharing, and learning green solutions. Furthermore, she is devoting her life to creating and nurturing eco-activists to be empowered to share the solutions of hope. Beyond that, Sara is dedicated to making every school the center of green solutions, within every community across the nation and ultimately the world.

Sara's Tip

Composting is an easy way to recycle organic matter (anything that was once living) like leaves, grass, and kitchen scraps to create nutrient-rich soil to grow more food. Many Americans are disconnected from the natural cycle of our planet. Composting reminds us that we are part of a cycle. When you eat food that is grown from soil, the leftovers can be put into a barrel, soil, or a composter with other organic matter in a 50/50 ratio. You need 50 percent brown material (sawdust, wood chips, dry leaves, shredded paper) and 50 percent green (fresh stuff, like kitchen scraps). Then the compost needs to be turned and mixed with water and oxygen. The compost will get hot because all the living things (fungus, bacteria, and invertebrates, i.e., "FBI") in it are eating away, which effectively decomposes your "waste." The more the FBIs eat, the hotter the pile gets, and in two to six months, depending on how hard the FBIs work, you'll have new and enriched soil to start planting new food.

DON'T put meat, heavy oils, citrus rinds, pet feces, or cheese in the compost. They will attract rats and insects, which are vectors of disease. Also, make sure not to add any invasive weeds because you'll just help boost the spread of unwanted species of plants. And if you keep turning it regularly, and adding water and wood chips, it should not smell bad at all!

CHAPTER 5

THE GROWERS AND GROCERS

Sustainable School Farmer

Amelia
Marstaller

Age: 17
Hometown:
Freeport, Maine

MEET AMELIA AND HER CAUSE

My name is Amelia Marstaller. I'm seventeen years old, and I live in Freeport, Maine. If you love the outdoors as much as I do, growing up in Maine is a special privilege. The air is fresh, the sky is filled with stars, and there is an abundance of locally grown food to eat. I like nothing more than taking a bite out of a fresh piece of fruit that I've grown myself or receiving produce grown by my neighbor. Food connects people, and being a "people person" with a passion for fresh food, I have been lifelong friends with the local farmers. They taught me how to grow food and, more important, how to show others that good, healthy food is essential to every community.

THE FUNKY CHICKEN

In 2005, I enrolled as a high school freshman at Emma Willard School, a boarding school in upstate New York. Soon after my arrival, I was eating a plate of chicken and vegetables in the dining hall, but my dinner tasted pretty funky. I suspected that it might not be fresh. I talked to the kitchen staff and was disappointed to discover that the cafeteria's offerings were not organic and, in fact, were full of preservatives. Also, our food supplies were being trucked in from thousands of miles away. Why were we shopping for groceries long distance when the countryside of upstate New York was covered with lush farms that were growing a wide assortment of fruits and vegetables? Not only was this system taxing the environment, the chemical

residue and synthetic hormones in preservative-treated produce and factory-farmed dairy and meat were damaging to my health and to that of my fellow students. It was a recipe for disaster, and I became determined to make some healthy changes to this menu!

Before I could make my case to the school administration, kitchen staff, and student body, I had to make sure I had my facts in order. I needed to convince everyone that organic food is better for us and better for the Earth because it is farmed without the use of harmful pesticides or herbicides. Organically raised animals are better because the animals must have access to the outdoors, and no synthetic hormones or antibiotics can be used to increase the amount of product. When I searched the Internet for data on the environmental impact of importing our food from other areas, I learned that most Americans live about 60 miles from an apple orchard, but typically, the apples bought at the supermarket travel 1,726 miles between the orchard and that store. That's farther than driving from Portland, Maine, to Miami, Florida! We were wasting fuel and polluting the air by transporting food to our school. I knew I had to do something to change this, so I presented the facts

Diane Hatz

**Founder/Director, Sustainable Table;
Executive Producer, *The Meatrix***

Like Amelia, supporting independent and family farms is important to grown-up green girl Diane Hatz. In fact, it's her job!

Diane Hatz develops creative projects to raise awareness and educate people about the sustainable food and agriculture movement and problems caused by factory farms. Diane is deeply committed to sustainability and helping to build a community through food. To raise awareness, Diane produced the award-winning animated films *The Meatrix, The Meatrix II: Revolting,* and *The Meatrix II 1/2.* These comical activist viral videos

have received almost 1 billion hits on www.youtube.com and have been translated into thirteen languages, proving that food really is an international issue. Diane is also the founder of the Eat Well Guide (www.eatwellguide.org), a great resource of family farms, restaurants, and other outlets for locally grown food.

Diane's Tip:

It's important to consider how recombinant bovine growth hormone (rBGH), which is injected into cows to increase their milk production, is not only a concern for your health but its use has a direct effect on the environment. According to Food and Water Watch (www.foodandwaterwatch.org), cows injected with rBGH need more feed to produce milk at such demanding levels, which means more feed needs to be grown and more pesticides released into the atmosphere. Planting, pesticide sprays, harvest, and transport pollute the soil and water. Around 10 billion pounds of nitrogen fertilizer, in addition to other pollutants, are introduced into fields and waterways every year to feed confined animal feeding operations (CAFO) cows. Encourage your parents to choose rBGH-free dairy products. You can find a list of rBGH-free products at the Sustainable Table Web site—www.sustainabletable.org.

www.sustainabletable.org

to the administration, and they encouraged me to head a task force on the issue. So I created the Emma Willard Sustainable Life Community Service Group and recruited a team of students who were determined to educate our community on the environment and committed to bringing local and organic food into our dining hall.

AMELIA'S SCHOOL GOES ORGANIC AND LOCAL

As a group, we approached our kitchen manager to offer more organic items in the dining hall. He was enthusiastic as long as we stayed within a budget. Organic options cost more, but the kitchen manager found ways of cutting other expenses and juggling the menu options to cover the increase. For instance, the kitchen now offers organic juice only at breakfast instead of offering commercially produced juice all day. By doing this type of shifting, we were able to provide hormone-free milk, organic bread, organic salad dressing, organic tea, and organic salad greens in our dining hall. The administrators listened to us and responded positively. I learned that, sometimes, you just need to ask for what you want.

Introducing locally grown food in our dining hall turned out to be a greater challenge. Our school's food service provider is an enormous company that orders large quantities of food from companies all over the country. This makes buying locally from small-scale farmers a huge shift in policy for the company, and very soon into our initiative, our group was up against some barriers. What has been important to remember is that we cannot expect change to happen overnight. Little steps toward our goal are great strides in terms of the local food movement.

When we learned there were so many restrictions on what the kitchen could buy locally, we looked for other ways to connect our community to the food we consume. We decided to grow our own food right on campus! We began by seeking the help of local farmers, who helped us plant our very own garden filled with all sorts of fruits and vegetables. I was particularly proud of this milestone because it was the first food grown and served at my school. And the first time we enjoyed our homegrown fresh and delicious vegetables was the most rewarding experience. I savored every bite! Although most of the local food we have at Emma Willard comes from our garden, we were able to bring in a few items from other local producers. We have organic pizza dough for weekly pizza day, and we made sure that every one of the apples in our cafeteria comes from a local orchard less than twenty miles away!

AMELIA GETS HER HANDS DIRTY AT DENISON FARM

I enjoyed working in our school's garden so much that I decided to spend the summer working at the nearby Denison organic farm. It's a lot of hard work and a lot of fun, too! I have learned so much more about organic farming from the Denisons. Organic farmers have the Earth's best interest at heart. They use methods that maintain the health and productivity of the soil while preserving the intricate web of life that exists in the field. When food is grown with chemicals and pesticides, the soil is stripped of its fertility, reducing its

ability to produce quality crops the following year. The job of an organic farmer is to take care of the Earth by using only nonharmful products to grow food.

Not only do I work at the Denison Farm, but I also travel with them to the Troy Waterfront Farmers Market to help sell their produce. One of my favorite things is the big display of fresh herbs right next to the cashbox (they form the farmers market equivalent to the candy-lined checkout aisle). These herbs give off the most glorious aroma, and sometimes I just have to stop and smell the basil. The great news is that you don't have to be a farmer to grow these herbs. You don't even have to have a garden. All you need is a sunny windowsill! Basil, thyme, cilantro, parsley, and mint can be grown indoors with the right amount of sunlight.

The farmers market is also a great place where community members can connect with the farmers who grow their food. Talking to the farmers about their products will help you understand the value of buying from the producer instead of from the store. It is also a good way to see what kind of food is produced seasonally in your region. If you are not sure where your local farmers market is, visit www.localharvest.org, type in your state and zip code, and you will find not only your local farmers markets but also local orchards, u-pick berry farms, food co-ops, and restaurants that feature local foods!

It can be difficult to get to a farmers market every week, and sometimes grocery stores are the convenient way to go. If you do shop at a grocery store, encourage your parents to purchase food from the organic and local aisles. Typically you can find organic and local eggs, meats, fish, milk products, and maybe a dessert or two! Buying even a few products that are organic and locally grown is a great way to support local farms and a healthy lifestyle.

WHAT'S COOKING IN AMELIA'S FUTURE?

With my experience, I hope to be a resource for starting farmers markets and for schools that want to have lunches made up of local food instead of frozen and packaged food. I want to reconnect people with the farmers who produce their food, a connection that has been lost as food becomes more mechanized. People need to invest in nearby growers and to forgo carbon-heavy produce from other countries. Not only is this essential to reducing the carbon footprint of food production, but it also has strong links to issues of humanity, such as safer, preservative-free food and an increased awareness of where our food comes from. The value of connecting people drives me to believe that the local movement can move us forward to a sustainable and unified future.

Amelia's RECIPE FOR SUPER-DUPER GREEN PESTO

This is a great pesto for pasta, pizza, or as a dip for bread. And all ingredients are easy to get from your local farmers market.

NOTE: makes about 3/4 cup

INGREDIENTS:

1 tablespoon pine nuts

2 cups basil leaves (1 bunch)

2 garlic cloves, smashed

6 tablespoons freshly grated Parmigiano-Reggiano cheese

6 tablespoons extra-virgin olive oil

Salt

DIRECTIONS:

1. In a small skillet, toast the pine nuts over moderate heat, stirring until golden (about five minutes). Transfer to a plate to cool.

2. In a blender or food processor, pulse the pine nuts with the basil, garlic, and cheese until finely chopped. While the machine is on, drizzle in the olive oil and puree until smooth. Season with salt, and your pesto is finished!

Ellen Page

FOR ACTRESS AND ECO-ACTIVIST ELLEN PAGE, GOING GREEN MEANS GROWING YOUR OWN FOOD!

Did Amelia's story make you hungry for change? Want to help make sustainable, organic food available for you and your loved ones? If you're the type of girl who loves digging her hands in the soil (or if you're interested in becoming one), there's no better way to spread your enthusiasm for healthy eating than by sharing it with your friends. My tip is to throw a planting party! It really doesn't matter if you live in the country or in a city because you can host an indoor gardening party or an outdoor celebration. All you need is to gather up some empty egg crates (for growing seedlings that can be transplanted later), or pots (with holes in the bottom), dirt or compost, and a few little shovels or even large spoons. Pick up some certified organic seed packets at a gardening store or from a Web site like www.seedsofchange.com. When choosing seeds for your planting party, it's important to make sure they are NOT genetically modified (GMO). Hybrid or GMO seeds are sterile, and less nutritious, and since they don't reproduce, they actually harm the biodiversity of our food sources. And, using GMO seeds supports a vicious and expensive cycle that forces farmers to buy new seed every year rather than following the ancient tradition of collecting and cleaning seeds after a harvest and saving them to be replanted to grow into more produce year after year. Certain natural strains of seeds have long histories, having been recycled by farmers for over 150 years, and we want to preserve them just the way they are. I don't need to grow a tomato that is square so that it fits better in supermarket packaging or that has a shelf life of sixty days. I like my food to be fresh and simple and pure. And make sure that you pick vegetables or herbs that can grow in

CERTIFIED ORGANIC

NO GMO NO GMO NO GMO NO GMO

a confined space, and that don't need much care other than a little sunshine and water. Some good seed choices would be peppers, heirloom or cherry tomatoes, or simple herbs such as sage or marjoram.

Gather together your green-minded friends and divvy up the seeds and other supplies. It's a good idea to make enough copies of the planting and care instructions on the back of the seed packets for each aspiring farmer. Make sure only one type of seed gets planted in each container.

Send each friend home with their own little "farm" and stay in touch to see how everyone's plants are faring. If you use egg crates, you will have to transplant the seedlings to larger pots when they get to be about two inches high.

When your veggies or herbs ripen, you can cook up a feast or make a great salad from the produce you've grown. That just gives you and your friends one more reason to get together!

After picking your produce and making a delectable salad from veggies you've grown with your own hands, you can keep the cycle going by cleaning your seeds and starting all over again by replanting next year. For more information on how to clean seeds, check out www. seedsofchange.com.

Anyone can start a little garden of their own! It's a great, fun way to get your friends excited about growing their own veggies, herbs, and even edible flowers!

www.seedsofchange.com

Urban Green Space

Araceli Tlatoa

Age: 15
Hometown:
Los Angeles,
California

MEET ARACELI AND HER CAUSE

I'm Araceli. I'm fifteen, and whenever I tell people I'm from South Central, L.A., they give me a worried look. I can tell they're thinking of gangs, gunshots, and graffiti. And I don't blame them. I've seen lots of kids get into trouble or end up in jail as a result of joining gangs, drinking, and doing drugs. But my experience has been totally different, thanks to the South Central Farm (www.southcentralfarmers.com).

My parents are from Puebla, Mexico, where they worked as farmers. When you grow up in a family of farmers, every day is a green day, as everyone becomes involved in the family business of growing and selling food. My mom's very traditional and very proud of her cooking, and she believes that the fruits and vegetables we eat have to be the best quality, as fresh as possible. My father grew up working the land. My parents have taught me the pride and satisfaction of knowing that the food on your dinner plate is the direct result of your own hard work.

Unfortunately, independent farmers in Mexico do not make much money. So my parents decided that they would seek a better life and emigrated to the United States, eventually settling in South Central, Los Angeles. For a family used to farming in an agricultural community, this was a big change! When they first drove into South Central, they saw more stores and buildings, and not a farm in sight!

Soon after they arrived, I was born. My upbringing has been much more typically American than Mexican. Our eating habits became very American; and like any other family, we would go to fast-food joints for hamburgers and milk shakes. Little by little my family left behind its agricultural roots and traditions.

A GARDEN HEALS A DAMAGED COMMUNITY AND A CITY GIRL BECOMES A FARMER

But things changed in 1991 when riots broke out in Los Angeles and devastated our community. South Central looked more like a war zone than a city. This part of town was badly burned and looted, and as people started to clean up, there was a feeling of despair and sadness among all my neighbors.

But out of the ashes and debris of the riots came a beacon of hope. In 1992, the City of Los Angeles granted South Central the use of a fourteen-acre plot of land to be made into a community garden. The garden was divided into family plots, and my dad was one of the first to line up for a plot. For the next twelve years, I had the privilege of working our section of land alongside my parents. I learned about our family's long tradition of organic farming in Mexico, and I was able to reconnect with my culture. I was proud to continue the indigenous Mexican tradition of organic farming.

The South Central Farm was the largest urban farm in the United States. Not only was I able to discover more about my roots, but I connected with more than 350 families

from different countries, different backgrounds, and different ways of life. I was very shy about talking to other people, but the more I showed up every day to work the land, the more people I met, and the more confident I became. I learned how to talk to different people and made lots of friends. I looked forward to heading to the farm after school every day or on the weekends. I was very proud of the work we were doing, and grateful to have such a beautiful and safe place to go to.

The farm was very much a family environment, an alternative to everyday life in the 'hood. Most of the other kids on the farm were from my neighborhood or my school. As the garden began to grow and bear fruits and vegetables, crime actually decreased in the area. Kids like my brothers and sister and me could run around and

Noa Lewis

Sunny-Side-Up Pizza Oven

Have more fun in the sun with a solar cooker

I'm Noa Lewis, I'm eleven years old, and I live in Cheviot Hills, California. I love to cook, as does everyone in my family, and it's not enough for our meals to be fresh and organic. I like to experiment with cooking methods that are also energy efficient. Why heat up a whole oven and expend a lot of energy for just one slice of pizza when there's a sunny alternative? How about making a solar oven out of a pizza box! Go to www.solarnow.org/pizzabx.htm for directions for making and using solar heat to cook up some healthy snacks. And it's a great green activity to do with kids you babysit that will also educate them on the power of solar energy. I learned how to make this oven while attending the Catalina Environmental Leadership Program at Catalina Island Camps (www.celp.net).

Noa and her brother, Max.

www.celp.net

119

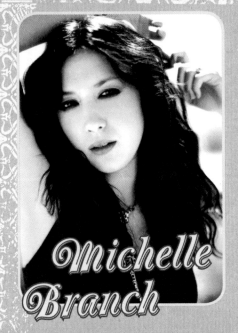

Michelle Branch

FOR SINGER AND SONGWRITER MICHELLE BRANCH, BEING GREEN MEANS SUPPORTING HER LOCAL FARMERS.

Did you know that the average American meal travels over 1,500 miles to get to your dinner plate, contributing great quantities of carbon dioxide emissions to the atmosphere in the process? Fresh is best, so I try not to buy food produced on some faraway factory farm. But sometimes it's just too complicated wondering where your food is coming from (and what's possibly in it!). Something that has really inspired me is that I try to eat locally whenever possible. When I buy my eggs, milk, butter, fruit, or greens, I try to find farmers near me whom I can support. The food is always loads fresher, it's great for the local economy, and there is something so romantic about getting your food straight from the source. To find out more about sustainable agriculture in your community, please check out www.localharvest.org/csa/.

www.localharvest.org/csa

play in the garden, and our parents didn't worry. We were free, and we were safe! This is how I grew up on a farm in the middle of urban South Central.

All the food we grew was organic—just like my mom and dad had done in Mexico. In the inner-city communities, a lot of people don't have access to organic food or information about what it means to eat organic food. One of the goals of the South Central Farmers has been to educate people on the benefits of eating organic food, to promote healthy eating habits, and to help fight health problems such as obesity. We did this by holding festivals at the farm, with food and music. We passed out flyers explaining the benefits of eating fresh, organic food. I encouraged my friends at school to eat less fast food and brought them to the farm to see and taste the diversity of fruits and vegetables we were growing. It was very exciting to see my friends become interested in learning about where their food came from and questioning if their food was organic or if it was grown with chemicals.

THE FARM IS LOST BUT NOT FORGOTTEN

The South Central Farm, or "the garden" as we called it, flourished for twelve years. It provided food, culture, and a source of pride to the community. But the land had been granted to the farmers only temporarily, and when a change in local politics happened, the land was sold and the farmers were evicted. I was very upset when this happened, and so were the other farmers. But rather than give in, the farmers decided to do something. We organized to protest the sale and legally appeal the eviction—and I was a part of this fight.

The struggle to save the South Central Farm got a lot of attention and support from artists and activists like Joan Baez, Willie Nelson, Daryl Hannah, and Rage Against the Machine's Zach de la Rocha. Our fight became a front-page newspaper story and received national coverage, with reporters visiting the farm daily. I became inspired, and learned how to fight for what matters most to me. I was among the farmers who spoke before the City Council to protest the unfair way the land was sold. We made our presentation and explained what the farm meant to us and how important it was to the community. But despite all our best efforts, we lost the South Central Farm, and the largest urban farm in the country was soon bulldozed. Although there have been plans to build a warehouse on this land, to this day, the lot remains empty and unused.

South Central Farmers' Cooperative
USDA Certified Organic Farm Fresh Vegetable
www.southcentralfarmers.com
(800) 249-5240

Join ou

THE TRADITION CONTINUES

Even though it was heartbreaking to lose this land, we did not give up. The South Central Farmers purchased land in Buttonwillow, California, where we continue raising organic produce. Although this new farm is far from my neighborhood, we believe in the need to bring fresh, organic food to the inner city, and we hold farmers markets in South Central. We now have booths in farmers markets throughout Los Angeles, and I love going on the weekends to help sell the fruits and vegetables. Our produce really does taste better than what you buy in the grocery store. I think that's because it's grown with so much heart.

Meredith Alexander

Founder, Milk and Bookies and Acme Sharing Co.

Like many of the other girls in this book, grown-up green girl Meredith Alexander is all about getting the green word out through entertaining and educational and healthy activities that engage the whole family and greater community. Meredith creates environmentally conscious events and activities that bring kids and their parents together to have fun while doing good.

Meredith Alexander lives in Los Angeles and is determined to leave the world a smidgen better than she found it. She is the founder of Milk and Bookies (www.milkandbookies.org), which teaches the importance of giving back to the community. Meredith also writes the blog Acme Sharing Company (www.acmesharing .com), where you can find fun, meaningful activities to do with the whole family.

Meredith's Tip:

GREEN BABYSITTING

Have an eco-friendly and organic lemonade stand with the kids you babysit.

You will need:

• Organic lemonade from concentrate
• 9-ounce clear biodegradable cups made of corn (they look like plastic party cups). (You can purchase these at www.treecycle.com.)
• Recycled paper napkins
• Make a stand out of recycled cardboard.
• All-natural (homemade or store-bought) cookies (you can bake these with your kids).

Now that you are ready for business, sell, sell, sell! And after you make some profit, choose a charity where you'd like to donate your hard-earned cash. For ideas on this, go to www.markmakers.org or www.youthgive.org.

www.markmakers.org

www.milkandbookies.org

www.youthgive.org

www.acmesharing.com

123

WHAT'S NEXT FOR ARACELI?

I would like to see more urban areas starting their own community farms. An edible urban garden is so beneficial to everyone. Not only does it bring together families, friends, and neighbors in a fun and delicious way, but it promotes healthy living and helps the air quality, too! I will keep working with my family at their booth at the farmers market. But the South Central Farmers can always use volunteers, so if you're in the area, you're invited to join us and pitch in!

 Araceli's TIP

Protect and help preserve family farms by shopping at your local farmers market. And when shopping at your local farmers market, don't forget to bring a reusable shopping bag or box, take your time to browse, and ask lots of questions! Don't be afraid to try new veggies or fruits. If you're not sure how to cook them, ask.

Zoe Nathan

Organic Chef, Rustic Canyon Wine Bar and Seasonal Kitchen and Huckleberry Cafe & Bakery

Zoe Nathan is a rising pastry star at Rustic Canyon Wine Bar and Seasonal Kitchen and the founder, with her husband restaurateur Josh Loeb, of Huckleberry Cafe in Santa Monica, California. At eighteen, Zoe started her career at Mario Batali's restaurant, Lupa, in New York City. And today, she continues to follow Mario's groundbreaking commitment to sustainable cooking and making food choices that consider environmental impact. She has made a name for herself with her salty-sweet and eco-healthy baking style. Zoe believes it is important to know the faces of the farmers she buys her fruit and other ingredients from, so you can find her shopping at the Santa Monica Farmers Market every Wednesday and Saturday. And each week she serves an array of desserts and other treats to eager customers from all around town.

Zoe's Recipe
WHOLE WHEAT SHORTBREADS

INGREDIENTS:
9 ounces butter, room temperature
1/2 teaspoon salt
1 cup and 2 tablespoons all-purpose flour
1/2 cup whole wheat flour
1/3 cup cornstarch
1/4 cup sugar

BAKING INSTRUCTIONS:
1. Preheat the oven to 350 degrees.
2. Mix the butter, salt, and sugar until light and fluffy.
3. Add the flours and the cornstarch to the mixture and mix until incorporated. Flatten out the dough and put in the refrigerator for twenty minutes to cool.
4. When slightly cooled, roll out on a floured surface to 1/4-inch thick, and cut with cookie cutters; when they are all cut, put in the freezer for at least twenty minutes.
5. Bake in the oven until slightly browned around the edges, remove from the oven, and quickly sprinkle with sugar.
6. Let cool before removing from the tray.

www.huckleberrycafe.com

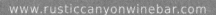

www.rusticcanyonwinebar.com

125

Zoe's Tip

IN LIEU OF GIFTS, PLANT A GARDEN!

For my wedding in January 2008, my husband Josh and I thought about what we might want for gifts, but not much came to us except for a single dream we've had—to transform our home's front and back yards into a beautiful edible organic garden. We devised a plan that included digging up our backyard driveway and planting numerous rows of organic foods, including lettuces, tomatoes, citrus trees, blueberry bushes, and even striped figs. Then we asked our wedding guests and families to consider donating to our garden account in lieu of gifts. A little over a year later, we are able to pick fresh herbs and produce right from our own yard. Nothing could be fresher than that!

If you are in a position to be receiving gifts but are not sure what you want to get, consider helping transform an outdoor space into an edible oasis by asking others to make a gift to your "garden" account. It's very easy to set up at www.paypal.com. Imagine receiving a gift that you can then turn around and give back to others by having your generous friends over for dinner made from your own organic produce!

126

CHAPTER 6

THE DEFENDERS OF AIR, LAND, AND WATER

Clean Air Adovocate

Erica Fernandez

Age: 17
Hometown:
Oxnard, California

MEET ERICA AND HER CAUSE

My name is Erica Fernandez. I'm seventeen years old, and I live in Oxnard, California. I was born and raised in Michoacán, Mexico, surrounded by the beauty of nature. My parents are farmworkers, and I grew up in the *campo*, or countryside, helping them in the fields along with my brother and my four sisters. Very few people in the *campo* had the privilege of owning a car, so we never really worried about air pollution.

But then my family moved to the United States when I was ten, and here it was just the opposite. It seemed like everyone drove a car, and the air was polluted. All I could smell was the stench of exhaust fumes. Soon after, I started having trouble breathing whenever I played or exercised. My parents took me to the doctor, who said that I had symptoms of asthma. I was given an inhaler, which helped, but I still worried every time I played sports that I would have an asthma attack. To make matters worse, my father had many health complications and also began suffering from respiratory problems. It was the air that was making us both sick. How were we to survive in a place with such polluted air? Something had to be done.

A PERSONAL HEALTH PROBLEM BECOMES A PUBLIC CAUSE

I was twelve when my passion for helping people and protecting the environment began. I learned about a company that wanted to build a natural gas facility near my hometown, which would create more air pollution and contribute to global warming. It would emit more than 280 tons of harmful pollutants into our air each year, no doubt aggravating my health problems as well as my dad's and others'. This foreign corporation was putting money and profit above our community's health. I was outraged. The people who would be most affected were low-income Latinos living in the area, many of whom were unaware of what was happening and unaware of the health and environmental dangers of the proposed plant. I knew I had to take action.

The first thing I needed to do was to educate myself on the issue. For the next month, I learned as much as I could about the proposed plant. I attended a community meeting and learned that the facility would send a thirty-six-inch pipeline through fifteen miles of low-income neighborhoods, which would require the destruction of houses in the surrounding areas. The more I learned about the plant, the more I realized that it would destroy the land and the air of my community if we did not do something to stop it. Every day that I had trouble breathing as I played soccer, or watched my dad struggle to breathe, it was clear that I had to seize the moment.

I began attending regular weekly meetings of a group called Central Coast Alliance United for a Sustainable Economy (CAUSE). Our goal was to fight the company that was seeking permits from the California State Lands Commission to grant the land to build the facility. Over the next four years, I became very involved in all of their activities and

www.coastalalliance.com

worked tirelessly to spread the message that the facility would ruin our air quality. If we succeeded here, we would then try to convince the California Coastal Commission that the facility did not meet our state's environmental standards. The final step would be to convince the governor to veto the project altogether so that there would be no hope for the company to proceed with their plans. We had no idea how successful or how far we could go, but we would do our best. I was passionate about defending the right of

every person in our community to have clean air to breathe.

In order to succeed, we had to build awareness and let people know how urgent and important it was to keep the natural gas facility out of our community. It really was a matter of life or death for people like my father and me, since we already suffered from compromised respiratory systems. We led an

educational campaign to raise awareness. At first, there were very few of us working on this campaign, and it was not easy to recruit people to the cause. People didn't see how we could succeed against such a powerful, multinational corporation. And many were skeptical about the problems; air is not something you can hold in your hand and show people. We met with people in the community and did a lot of outreach to community groups and organizations. And with each presentation, we asked those present to introduce us to new networks of like-minded people and organizations we could approach for support. I learned about choosing my words wisely and speaking with passion and conviction. I saw that my words had an effect on people, and little by little, I was able to inspire my friends and family to learn about the issue and get involved. I fought apathy with passion for this issue, and my enthusiasm and commitment led the way for others to join the fight.

In 2007, the fourth year of our campaign, there was a hearing at which the California State Lands Commission would vote to grant the land to the corporation. We had only three months to prepare for that hearing. During that time, we hoped to get at least five hundred people together to express our concerns and to try to delay the project. It meant daily calls to people on our list to remind them about the hearing.

I helped contact the media, calling radio and television stations. At first I was nervous calling them—I didn't have that much confidence. But they were very supportive. We did interviews and invited the press to come to different meetings to cover the topic. I passed out flyers, organized more than three hundred students in my high school, and went door-to-door in the areas that were going to be most affected. Even on the day of the hearing I was knocking on doors, and there were still people who hadn't heard of the project. I needed to change that.

ERICA SPEAKS FOR PEOPLE

When it came time for the hearing, CAUSE chose five individuals to represent the people and give their testimony. I was chosen to represent our local youth. I would have only ninety seconds to make my point. I was afraid they weren't going to listen to me because I was young, but I spoke from my heart.

"We, the young people of Ventura County, are the ones who are going to live with this polluting project, not you. Do we deserve another grossly polluting project in Oxnard? Do we really need to host another power plant? Is my hometown not worth having beautiful beaches and beautiful views of the ocean? If you allow this project to come into my community, our future will be dependent on a company which has become wealthy at any cost. Do they live here? No. Do they vote here? No. Do their children go to school with me? No. Would you allow us to become their experiment?"

When I finished, the commissioners clapped, something uncommon in this venue, and then they went off to vote. I was very happy when Lieutenant General John Garamendi, who chaired the meeting, congratulated me. He said that when he was sixteen, he wouldn't have been out doing something like this. I went outside to see how many people had come to lend their support to our cause. We had hoped for five hundred and there were more than three thousand supporters gathered. Everyone wore blue shirts in solidarity, and they were chanting and waving signs. There were people of all ages and backgrounds, all united for one purpose. After ten hours of deliberation, the commission voted and we won 2 to 1—the land grant was denied.

A VICTORY, BUT IT WASN'T OVER YET

A few days later there was a second hearing— this one with the California Coastal Commission. Although the State Lands Commission at the previous hearing had already denied the land grant, if the corporation succeeded at this hearing, it would give them a reason to find another way to build a natural gas facility. The issue at this hearing was whether or not the proposed plant met state and federal coastal-protection laws. I was asked to speak, and again I spoke from my heart. After my speech, a ninety-year-old lady came to me, crying. She told me she had lost hope and had been planning to cede her chance to speak because she thought no one would listen to her. But hearing my speech inspired her to address the crowd, and she did a fantastic job! It felt so good to know that I was making a difference by speaking up. That day, the commissioners voted unanimously 12 to 0, in our favor, confirming that the facility did not meet the state's environmental standards.

The next challenge was getting Governor Arnold Schwarzenegger to veto the project. We were not sure how he would vote, so we intended to do everything we could to make sure he voted in our favor. We wrote letters and made calls every day asking him to save our coast. And in the end, all of our hard work paid off. He vetoed the project!

ORGANIZING A COMMUNITY TAKES A LOT OF HARD WORK AND COMMITMENT

I learned a lot about how to get people motivated and involved in a campaign. In 2008, I invited Jane Goodall to come speak at my high school. She encouraged all of us to take action and make our world a better place. People will take action when they understand that their future is in imminent danger. And there's a lot of hard work involved in making the community aware of an issue and organizing them to bring about change. This includes creating posters, making calls, providing security at the rallies, and hanging up leaflets in the neighborhood. For our campaign, it was crucial to gather contact information for everyone who attended so that

we could remind them to come to the next meeting and bring more supporters. The key to our success was diligence, perseverance, and constant attention to details.

THE SKY'S THE LIMIT FOR ERICA

Education is very important to me, and I believe it is the key to effecting social change. I want to serve minorities and champion the causes of other underrepresented groups. I see the well-being of my community as my own well-being. One person alone can go only so far. It was when we united as a community that we were successful.

I follow the words of my personal hero and role model, activist César Chávez, who said, "Once social change begins, it cannot be reversed. You cannot uneducate the person who has learned to read, you cannot humiliate the person who feels pride, and you cannot oppress the people who are not afraid anymore. We are the future and the future is ours."

Erica's TIP

Stand up and fight for what you believe in! Tell your friends, parents, teachers, and colleagues, and then go straight to the top—to the government; make politicians listen to you and act on behalf of the people. Find a cause that excites you, join the movement, and let it be known. As Gandhi said: **BE THE CHANGE YOU WISH TO SEE IN THE WORLD!**

Sharon Smith

Program Director for the New Leaders Initiative and Brower Youth Awards, Earth Island Institute

In 2007, Erica received a prestigious award from the Earth Island Institute for her activist work. Sharon Smith played an important role in giving her this honor.

Sharon Smith launched her career in environmental advocacy in 1999 with a fellowship with Green Corps, the field school for environmental organizing. Today Sharon works at the Earth Island Institute, an environmental group

founded by the famous conservationist David Brower. She coordinates the awards program honoring young environmental leaders in the United States and Canada for their outstanding activism and achievements. The awards shine a spotlight on rising leaders between the ages of

thirteen and twenty-two, and encourage them to make activism a lifelong practice. Sharon connects these eco-heroes to resources, mentors, skill building, funding, workshops, and other opportunities to further their leadership development. Previously, Sharon was a driving force in Rainforest Action Network's national markets campaign victories. She worked extensively with student networks to achieve victories in pushing banks out of dirty energy projects and loggers out of old growth forests. In addition, Sharon led youth on extended wilderness backpacking and cross-country bike touring trips in the United States. To find out more about the Brower Youth Awards, visit www.broweryouthawards.org.

Sharon's Tip: How to Be an Activist

SPEAK FROM YOUR HEART: You don't need to use jargon and statistics. People will connect with you if you are honest, genuine, and sincere. Find your passion and share it with others.

USE YOUR YOUTH: You know all the cool places young people go—so spread the word at these untapped venues. Go to your favorite band's concert or hit up the local coffee shop.

DON'T BACK DOWN: Environmental leaders didn't get where they are by giving up. Your endless perseverance will impress people. It will happen—it just takes effort.

DELEGATE RESPONSIBILITIES: As fantastic as you are, you aren't Superwoman. Delegate responsibilities. It gives you a break and gets others invested in your cause.

ATTEND AN EVENT, CAUCUS, OR CONVENTION: Surround yourself with other inspired people, network with youth who are doing similar things, and learn from the experts on environmental issues. Take back that energy to reenergize your fight!

USE THE MEDIA: Local media are always looking for amazing community members to feature. So start with the local TV, radio, and newspapers and pitch the idea of a monthly green column or share your story with a reporter.

BE A YOUNG PHILANTHROPIST: Whether you work or get an allowance, put away a dollar a week and donate it to a cause that you care about. What goes around comes around. You can research various environmental charities at www.networkforgood.org.

HAVE FUN FUND-RAISING: Money doesn't bring happiness, but it is useful. Have fun when you fund-raise. Throw a party. Have a concert or a dance. Get all your friends to text an invitation to everyone in their contact lists. Just make sure to keep the carbon footprint of your activities to a minimum.

FOCUS ON THE POSITIVE: Your positive attitude will keep people going when you inevitably encounter obstacles. And of course, celebrate each and every green victory!

www.networkforgood.org

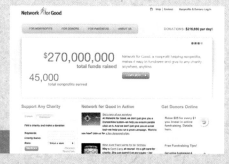

Defender of Sacred Land

Alberta Nells

Age: 18
Hometown:
Flagstaff, Arizona

MEET ALBERTA AND HER CAUSE

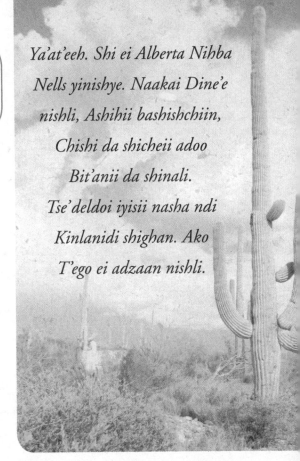

Ya'at'eeh. Shi ei Alberta Nihba Nells yinishye. Naakai Dine'e nishli, Ashihii bashishchiin, Chishi da shicheii adoo Bit'anii da shinali. Tse'deldoi iyisii nasha ndi Kinlanidi shighan. Ako T'ego ei adzaan nishli.

My name is Alberta Nihba Nells and I am eighteen years old. I am of the Dine' (Navajo) people of northern Arizona. I am of the Mexican (Wondering People) Clan and I am born for the Salt Clan. My maternal grandfather is of the Cheruca-hua Apache, and my pater-nal grandfather is of the Folding Arms Clan. I am from Hard Rock, Arizona (Navajo Nation), but I re-side in Flagstaff. I am a native Dine' woman.

In my culture, we are taught to appreciate and revere nature in a very special way. All things are sacred because everything—from a newborn baby to a blade of grass—has life. The preserva-tion of our indigenous values and way of life is inextricably tied to the preservation of our sacred lands. If we allow our sacred lands to be destroyed, what will become of our culture? As a young Native American woman in a modern world, I have turned to the ancient prayers, songs, and values of my people to find the inspiration to fight to protect my sacred homeland.

Four years ago, my community was shocked to learn that plans were being made to allow the development of a ski resort on the San Francisco Peaks, mountains that are held sacred by more than thirteen tribes in the Southwest, including my own tribe, the Dine'. The Dine' have four main sacred mountains, one to each direction; within these four mountains is our homeland, where we live. The plans for the ski resort included the use of reclaimed wastewater to make artificial snow on the peaks. This broke my heart. I am somewhat shy, but I could feel my shell cracking because I knew had to speak out against what I believed was an injustice against my people and the desecration of the earth we hold dear.

PRAYER, DIGNITY, AND A HINT OF REBELLION

Shortly after the development plans were approved, there was a community screening of the documentary film called *The Snowbowl Effect*, which explored the controversy. The film was written and directed by Klee Benally, a Native American filmmaker and founder of the Save the Peaks Coalition. I knew Klee from his extensive work in the community and his focus on helping indigenous youth address environmental and social justice issues through film and other media. When I expressed my anger and frustration to Klee, he encouraged me to attend the screening and address the audience afterward.

I had never done any public speaking, but I wanted to inspire those gathered to take action. I wanted them to know how important the mountains were to me and my people. As I spoke from the heart, I could see the audience tearing up. I had found my voice. It was the first of many screenings where Klee would invite me and other local young people to speak. We continued screening and speaking to the public for an entire summer, and when we went back to school, we decided to form Youth of the Peaks (YOTP) to keep the momentum of our movement.

The mission of Youth of the Peaks is to maintain this mountain for the coming generations, along with the culture that is indelibly tied to it. We want to keep it pure and uncorrupted for the next millennium and beyond. Native Americans have already lost so much of our land, culture, language, and traditions. It is up to younger members of the tribes to lead the people out of the darkness and put them back on the good road of life that our ancestors walked many years ago. We had ten enthusiastic people at our first Youth of the Peaks meeting, and everyone was ready to jump into the agenda. Youth of the Peaks was set in motion—with prayer, dignity, and a hint of rebellion.

It heartens me that with every event Youth of the Peaks hosts, we attract more supporters. We have effectively discouraged the resort from expanding on

the mountain. As members of YOTP, we must speak the words from our hearts. People were touched to see young Native Americans stand up for the people and land. We have found other ways of serving our community, including wood hauling for our elders, painting murals, planting, restoring gardens, conducting media training, organizing alcohol and drug prevention projects, hosting theatrical productions, learning the traditional ways from our elders, holding tribal summits, organizing music projects, and so much more. These experiences help our members envision a better future for themselves, something beyond the stereotypical life on a reservation.

WHAT'S NEXT FOR ALBERTA?

I enjoy working with people and I continue to make speeches on behalf of our cause. I speak at local events to share our story that indigenous people are still struggling to protect the sacred land that is our mother. I am blessed by the continued support of my family, and am grateful to those who inspired me and encouraged me to speak out. I am considering a career in filmmaking with an eye to using media to inspire and compel social change. I have been working with Outta Your Backpack Media, an organization that offers indigenous youth workshops and mentorship programs to develop media skills. With this training, I hope to use media to pursue social and environmental justice.

After people see my short films and hear me speak, they always thank me for my work and for my words. I tell them that the words I speak are not my own, they are the words of the Creator. What started out with ten students meeting in a classroom has grown so much over the past three years. We have supporters all over the country. We have made an impact. People see young Native Americans taking a stand in what they think is right for the land and people. It gives them hope that their great-grandchildren are going to be coming into a better world.

As a community, we need to work together. At Youth of the Peaks, we have a chant: "The people, united! We'll never be divided!" and that is the true spirit of our group. We are not alone. We need to respect ourselves, one another, and most important, the land.

Alberta's TIP

Each aspect of the environment, be it the trees that create oxygen or the bees that pollinate plants, is working cohesively to sustain itself and the elements that surround it. It's a daily lesson in how we as humans must relate to an environment that has long cherished and supported us. Just as I spoke out through my community, you can do the same. Get involved through your church, synagogue, mosque, or other community organization. Take advantage of their support to further a cause that matters to you!

The Greening of New Orleans

Jordan Sale

Age: 18
Hometown: Los Angeles, California

CREOLE QUEEN

MEET JORDAN AND HER CAUSE

I'm Jordan Sale, I'm eighteen, and I live in Los Angeles. But not too long ago, my heart became enamored of a very different city. When Hurricane Katrina hit New Orleans, I was deeply affected by news reports of the devastation. I was barely fifteen at the time and too young to participate as a volunteer in the cleanup and relocation efforts. I did what I could and collected clothes and raised funds for the victims, but I also vowed that when I came of age, I would find a way to help rebuild NOLA.

A CITY IN NEED OF GREEN HELPING HANDS

I got my chance during spring break of my senior year, when several members of my class joined a philanthropic mission sponsored by Habitat for Humanity International (HFHI) to help build homes in NOLA. Habitat for Humanity works to eliminate poverty and homeless- ness from the world and to make decent shelter a matter of conscience and action. It was one of the first organizations to come to NOLA's aid by bringing in volunteer crews to build shelters for its displaced residents. My friends and I were committed members of the environmental club at school and felt that the chance to work on this project was the opportunity of a lifetime. Not only would we be helping rebuild New Orleans, we would be building it back green, as the project incorporated cutting-edge sustain- able design and materials.

HFHI made arrangements with Global Green (GG) to have us work on the Holy Cross Project, a residential development designed by a green ar- chitect who won a contest judged by sustainable design advocate, GG supporter, movie star, and New Orleans homeowner Brad Pitt. The Holy Cross site is in NOLA's Lower Ninth Ward, a neighborhood that was completely ravaged by the hurricane. Build- ing homes for other people with your own hands is incredibly gratifying. At the end of every day on the building site, you can step away and look over this house that you built with your own two hands and with the help of a great group of new friends.

LIFE IN THE BIG EASY

The Global Green Holy Cross building site is a truly green development for affordable, sustainable housing and a school. As a teenager, I had not really thought about what goes into making a building green. The innovations that Global Green's architects and planners had come up with to save money, time, and the Earth's resources motivated me to think about all the elements that go into our shelters in general—our homes, schools, and community buildings. I walked through the site while GG administrators explained how they were starting from scratch, using nontoxic, renewable, and recycled building materials and designs. I was fascinated by the many benefits of green building. It made me wonder about the "green-ness" of my own home and school back in Los Angeles.

BRINGING THE GREEN BACK TO SCHOOL

When I returned home from my trip, I was so excited to get involved with Global Green and work on some green renovations in my own environment. My parents are extremely eco-conscious, but my enthusiasm renewed their enthusiasm to take our green house-hold to the next level. My dad has also been a huge source of inspiration to me, actively trying to use less water, conserving energy, and recycling. Together, we started a compost pile in our yard and have replaced most of our lightbulbs with compact fluorescent bulbs. Now that my home was on its way to being eco-friendly, I could focus on greening up my school.

I worked with the members of my school's Student Council to convince the school administration to make the environment more of a priority. Our school was undergoing a large construction project, and we were able to persuade the senior administrators to incorporate environmental initiatives, much like the ones I saw in New Orleans, into the new building. I also helped launch the Environmental Action Committee, which focused on a schoolwide effort for recycling, reduced paper usage, and reduced energy consumption. We had to consult with school administrators and looked at other schools for models on how to enact change on a campus.

Next, I made a short film, which I screened at school, that illustrated simple tips to help make the Earth a cleaner, safer, and healthier place. The response was so positive that I helped set up a green fashion show at school to keep my classmates excited about green living. The fashion show was modeled after *Project Runway,* and we gave our students a challenge to design clothes that were environmentally friendly. The student designers were so creative and green through and through! There were dresses made of recycled noncloth items, one designer gave our current uniform a green "upgrade," and there was even a gorgeous dress composed of trash bags. We made more than $60,000 and donated the proceeds. I know that I've left my school in great green hands as the younger girls working on these projects are as committed to promoting environmental awareness as I am.

WHAT'S NEXT FOR JORDAN?

Greening my home and school are just the beginning. I volunteer at Global Green's offices, helping with clerical support and guiding people through the many exhibits on green building in the lobby. I also man booths at events like the Venice Eco-Fest. We need to keep getting the word out and making people aware of all the things they can do in their homes and communities to green-up their world.

Jordan's TIP

I've learned so much working as an intern at Global Green. My best piece of advice is to become an intern at an office that works in the area of your interest. There is nothing comparable to what you'll learn just by being there, answering phones, meeting people, and interacting with the experts. So find a cause that excites you and become an intern to get hands-on experience and make a difference!

Summer Rayne Oakes

Model-activist; author of *Style, Naturally: The Savvy Shopping Guide to Sustainable Fashion & Beauty*

FOR AUTHOR, MODEL, AND ACTIVIST SUMMER RAYNE OAKES, BEING GREEN MEANS GETTING YOUR HANDS DIRTY!

Planting trees is one of the greatest ways to get involved in the environment. It's a simple action that makes you feel close to the Earth—and has so many other added benefits—from shading areas from the sun, holding the Earth intact, protecting our lands from floods, providing a habitat for wildlife, and storing CO_2. I head to Mozambique every year and work on restoring forest lands that have been lost to slash-and-burn and illegal logging. The benefits all around are undeniable.

My tip to you: Start a forest for your friends! Instead of buying birthday gifts, plant a tree in honor of your friend. Find out more at www.treepeople.org.

www.treepeople.org

149

Allison Wilkey

Assistant to President & CEO, Global Green

Allison Wilkey served as Jordan's mentor during her internship with Global Green.

A California native and environmental advocate since junior high school, Allison Wilkey joined Global Green after careers in the business and political worlds. Prior to this, Allison spent time in Washington, D.C.,

www.globalgreen.org

as an environmental paralegal at a top international law firm. Currently Allison provides high-level executive support to the president and CEO of Global Green USA, Matt Petersen, in addition to day-to-day management of the organization's regional committees.

Allison's Tip:

It's not uncommon to find that much of one's life experience has been shaped by one's teachers and personal interpretation of those teachings. My heart's path woke up after an enlightening Earth science class in the eighth grade, where I first learned of deforestation and global warming. And without conscious thought I knew that such issues were life-threatening, and it wasn't okay to let them be. Since that teaching and subsequent volunteer experience, I've never hesitated about my chosen place in the world and my intention to fight for our environment— the rights of it and all that exist within it. And because I was taught these values, it's clear that others must be educated, too . . . or else they may never learn. And we can't leave our future up to chance.

THERE ARE LOTS OF SIMPLE THINGS THAT ARE EASY TO DO TO MAKE YOUR HOME A LITTLE MORE GREEN!

1. Ask your parents to lower the thermostat. For every degree lowered, your heating costs are lowered 5 percent. Also, make sure to close your windows and

your fireplace if you have one; a lot of heat is lost through them and you could save more than 10 percent of your total energy by keeping these gaps sealed.

2. Turn off those lights when you leave the room, and be sure to use the energy-saving option on appliances that offer it.

3. Avoid being driven around; walk, take the bus, or ride your bike. Cars are responsible for roughly 60 percent of air pollution in big cities.

4. Switch to compact fluorescent lightbulbs, which are four times more energy efficient and have a life span that is ten times longer than incandescent lightbulbs.

5. Save water by asking your parents to use the automatic dishwasher and washing machine only for full loads. And make sure to have your parents check the faucets and pipes for leaks. Leaks waste water twenty-four hours a day, seven days a

week, and often can be repaired with just an inexpensive washer.

6. And the easiest tip to remember: Don't let the water run while you brush your teeth!

Visit www.globalgreen.org to get construction updates about the Holy Cross Project and to find out more about how you can help.

A Promise of Clean Water for All

Emily Welsh

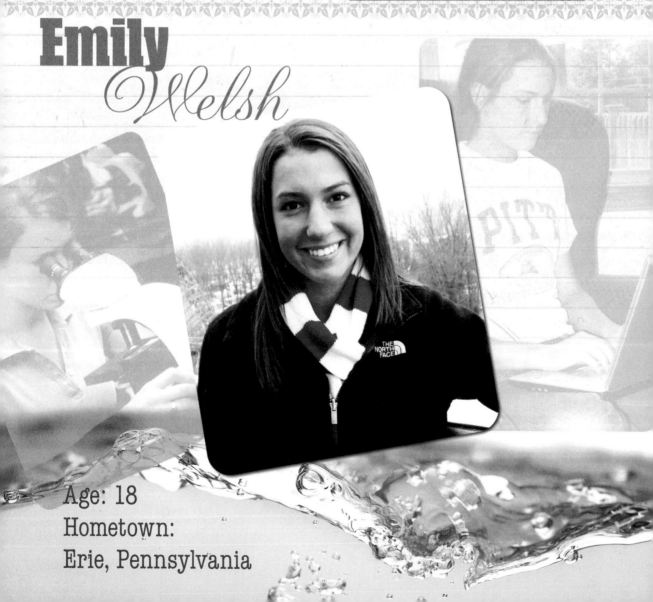

Age: 18
Hometown:
Erie, Pennsylvania

MEET EMILY AND HER CAUSE

I'm Emily Welsh. I'm eighteen, and I live in Erie, Pennsylvania. I have always been concerned about the welfare of others. I hear about an injustice or a social issue, and it clicks inside me; that's it—I just have to find a way to help. Volunteering is a big part of my life. I have performed more than a hundred hours of community service, and I especially enjoy being part of a team of people working together toward the greater good.

So when I first heard about the United Nations Children's Fund (UNICEF) (www.unicef .org) Tap Project from my mom, I had to find out more. The facts were shocking! More than 1 billion people worldwide do not have access to clean drinking water. It is a daily privilege that millions of people in the United States take for granted. In addition to the lack of access to clean drinking water, more than 2.6 billion people worldwide lack access to adequate sanitation. As soon as I read the research, I felt that familiar *click* and knew I had to do more. Maybe the Tap Project was a way for me to reach out to impoverished people across the globe from right here in my own hometown of Erie?

EMILY TAPS INTO A SOLUTION

UNICEF's Tap Project is an ingenious proposition—ask customers in restaurants to donate one dollar for each glass of tap water they normally get for free. The UNICEF Tap Project raises money to provide clean drinking water to children around the world by

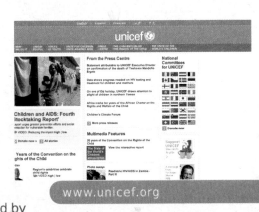

www.unicef.org

funding pumps, pipelines, testing kits, and training. Every dollar raised for the Tap Project means a child will have clean drinking water for forty days.

The Tap Project was first launched in Manhattan in 2007, and in 2008 it expanded to other cities, like Los Angeles, Dallas, New Orleans, Boston, and Atlanta (all major metropolitan centers much bigger than Erie). I really believe that a dollar is a small price to pay for the difference it will make in the lives of children elsewhere, and I knew that I would surely find other people in Erie who felt the same way. I contacted the organizers at the Tap Project's Web site to see if I could bring the project to Erie, and they agreed to support my efforts. They gave me the details of what the program would entail for prospective restaurants that agreed to participate. Then I asked my family for their support, and as always, they were instantly on board. So by the end of my first day on the campaign, we were a team of five, but I realized that I needed some kind of "official" affiliation with the city. That's when I contacted John Oliver, the CEO of Visit Erie, Erie's convention and visitors' bureau.

I explained the importance of the project to him, and he was eager to help. He also became the honorary chair of this event, which now meant that Erie was officially on board. The campaign takes place over one week and was scheduled to coincide with World Water Day on March 22, 2008. Mr. Oliver helped me identify more than three hundred restaurants in the area to send letters to asking for their support, and he also helped advertise the project through interviews with local media.

Emily Welsh, a senior at Mercyhurst Preparatory School, is attempting to raise money to provide drinking water to Third World countries.

Help on tap

Teen turns it on for UNICEF water fundraiser

We drafted a press release and held a press conference to get the word out quickly. People can't take part in an event if they don't know about it, so we made sure everyone in town heard about our plan. After I sent out the initial three hundred letters, I also made about fifty phone calls to follow up with the most promising candidates among the local restaurants and asked for their participation. I wrote up a script for phone solicitations that I would read from in order to be clear about what I was asking them to do.

Making cold calls is difficult, but if you have a compelling story to tell and do so in an organized and polite manner, most people will listen to you. Once they agreed, it was a simple online process to register restaurants in my city to be included in the event.

Although the event was widely publicized, I hit a wall—of chains, that is—when many of the restaurants I contacted were prevented from taking part because of corporate policies on fund-raising. They would have to get permission from their national headquarters, which would take much more time and effort. With only a few weeks to the campaign, there was no way I could get the chain restaurants on board in time.

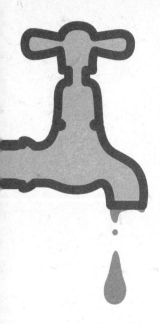

To make matters worse, I ran into some other challenges. Local restaurants were not as enthusiastic as I had hoped. With just days before the launch, not one restaurant had joined the cause. It was very disappointing, but I would not let this stop me. I focused on the facts: a child dies from water-related causes every fifteen seconds, and that adds up to approximately six thousand children dying from this problem every day (see www.tapproject.org for more). For just one dollar, a child would be provided with forty days of clean drinking water. It's a matter of life and death for these kids, and I knew that I could not give up. I put everything I had, all my passion for this project, into my solicitations, and my next call was a success. I had my first restaurant registered, and two more major restaurants also signed up to take part. While only three restaurants in the region eventually jumped on board, my call for humanitarian action was giving the people of Erie the power to effect change in the lives of others.

During the week of the campaign, my family made the commitment to eat at each of the three restaurants and pay for our tap water to set an example for others. The owners were so enthusiastic and kind, especially Chef Matthew Sarbak of Matthew's Trattoria. He made a point of coming to our table and sat down with me for about fifteen minutes to encourage me to keep the project going. He offered to host a group of his peers to drum up participation for the following year. He explained that restaurants are overwhelmed by local and national charity requests, and that there are just so many donations they

can make and still run a profitable business. Chef Matthew suggested that we should do a teach-in by phone with representatives from UNICEF and the Tap Project during his gathering of fellow chefs, to give them a chance to ask the experts more questions about the crisis. The more they know, the more likely they are to become involved.

In total, we raised $8,000 for the Tap Project in one week by serving Erie tap water with a touch of good karma. But, more important, we raised awareness. Many people have said to me that they didn't understand the desperate need for clean water in many nations around the world, and I think the more exposure the problem gets, the more others will do to reach out and help. Although this year's Tap Project did not bring in quite as much money in my city as we had hoped, it was a substantial kickoff year. I am confident that Erie will continue to support the project in greater numbers.

WHAT'S AHEAD FOR EMILY?

I want to make my humanitarian and environmental work be more directly connected

with those who need it. My work on the Tap Project has been a very instructive first step in helping me understand the issues and ethics of the international water crisis, and I'm thirsting to find more ways to help! You can find out more about the Tap Project at www.tapproject.org.

www.tapproject.org

Emily's TIP

Register at Disney's Friends for Change at www.disney.go.com/projectgreen and join your peers in a pledge to make small changes in your daily life—from fixing leaky drains to creating a composting system to installing energy-saving light bulbs. These small changes help preserve water and natural habitats and reduce waste and your negative contributions to climate change.

DISNEY FRIENDS FOR CHANGE
project green
©Disney

FOR ACTRESS SARAH JANE MORRIS, OF *BROTHERS & SISTERS*, BEING GREEN MEANS BEING ULTRACONSCIOUS EVERY DAY OF HER WATER AND ENERGY USAGE.

There are so many ways you can conserve energy, but I personally do things like ONLY using lights in the room I'm actually in and turning off all lights when I leave the house; unplugging my hair dryer, flat iron, cell phone charger, laptop charger, and other small appliances as soon as I finish using them (you'll forget later). I got a new TV (the first in nine years and gave my old one to a friend in need) and opted for the Philips eco-friendly flat screen that draws about as much power as a standard incandescent lightbulb. And although this isn't exactly an option for everyone, I drive a car powered by waste veggie oil! It's an old Mercedes I bought on eBay, and the diesel engine had a very easy conversion that made it possible to run on grease. It's only a part of the solution, but it certainly makes me drive with a smile on my face knowing that I'm doing something good for the planet. Of course, I still try to walk, ride my bike, or carpool whenever possible!

Water conservation is all about changing your habits, like turning off the hot before the cold, turning off the water while brushing your teeth, or brushing your teeth while you are waiting for the water to heat up to wash your face or shave. Don't rinse your dishes before they go in the dishwasher. And it's good to water houseplants from glasses of water that have been sitting out or that you are finished with. Try installing a low-flow showerhead (I got the Waterpik EcoFlow) and take quicker showers by just doing what you need to do to get clean rather than spacing out under the hot water for long periods of time. I try to remember how fortunate we are to have the luxuries we do—like clean hot water and electricity. Imagine what life would be like without them and know that someday that could be a reality if we don't start changing our habits now. Wouldn't you rather make changes on your own than have someone like the government ordering you to do it? I know I would!

CHAPTER 7

THE ENVIRONMENTAL SCIENTISTS AND GREEN ENGINEERS

CO$_2$

Wind Energy

Savannah Pope

Age: 16
Hometown:
New York, New York

MEET SAVANNAH AND HER CAUSE

I'm Savannah Pope, and when I was sixteen, I became concerned about the state of the environment. It happened to me over the course of a summer while I was living in New York City. I kept noticing trash, the everyday stuff that most of us throw away without thinking much about, and I could not stop thinking about what would become of all of it. I quickly became aware of the life cycle of every object I used each day, and any new objects I brought into my life had to be intelligently designed to be sustainable. Given our planet's limited resources, there had to be a better way of living.

I began researching current environmental issues, and soon enough I became an outspoken advocate of recycling. I then read about global warming, and was shocked how nobody I knew seemed to take an interest in the matter. But then I left New York for a much greener part of the country—Vermont. I was sure that moving to one of the most environmentally conscious states was going to bring me into a more like-minded group of peers.

SAVANNAH MEETS HER MENTOR

You can imagine my surprise when I started my new school and discovered that the "green trend" had not caught on. I needed to make people aware of the environmental problems we see every day and the ways we can fix them. I stood out like a green thumb, but only for

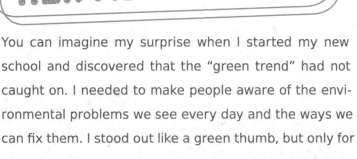

a while. Luckily, I enrolled in an environmental studies class with a teacher who changed my life. She became my role model, championing environmental causes and pushing to better the school against all faculty and student resistance.

A CONTEST TAILOR-MADE FOR A GREEN-MINDED GIRL

I was assigned a project in our environmental studies class: We were to look at different energy sources and study the pros and cons of each option. I studied wind energy, and I quickly became completely obsessed with it. I needed to know everything about the subject. Then my teacher notified me, and Rachel, another girl in my class who was also interested in alternative energy, about the Ben & Jerry's Lick Global

www.benjerry.com

Warming contest. It was an opportunity for high school students to win $2,000, a year's supply of ice cream, and some souvenirs signed by Al Gore from the documentary *An Inconvenient Truth*. These prizes were to be awarded to the students who presented the best proposal for a project that would reduce the onset of global warming and educate their community about the environment.

Rachel and I decided that we wanted to install a wind turbine on our school campus and design a community-friendly education system surrounding alternative energy. We presented the idea to our school headmaster, and initially there was not much interest. It really came down to aesthetics. The administration felt that a wind turbine would be an eyesore on campus.

This was unacceptable for Rachel and me. The administration was choosing beauty over helping preserve our Earth. We decided then and there that we would win the Ben & Jerry's contest and get enough positive publicity that it would make it difficult for our school administrators to turn us down. To our surprise, when word got out, our community was inspired when they saw how dedicated we were to coming up with a winning proposal. The administration took us seriously and committed to help us make this idea become a reality.

SAVANNAH READS EVERYTHING AND ANYTHING ON WIND ENERGY

We spent a long time researching our options to develop a solid plan. Our teacher opened up her house to us, and soon her place became a haven for countless hours of brainstorming, chocolate eating, and late nights spent writing the proposal. It was a lot to handle on top of schoolwork, but it was empowering. We were working together as a team toward a clear goal that was very important to all of us.

We took a lot of examples from nearby schools that had installed wind turbines, and we tried to gather as much information as we could from them, reviewing the positives and negatives of their experiences. We then contacted alternative energy engineers and spoke with them about which turbine model would be best for our site. Finally, we decided on a wind turbine that would cost approximately $53,000. We looked into all of the grants we could apply for, and developed a plan as to where we were going to get all this money. We contacted school alumni, the board of trustees, and environmentally conscious parents, some of whom promised to donate matching funds if we managed to win the Ben & Jerry's contest. We even met with representatives from the Vermont state senator's offices to get advice and feedback on state incentives.

After doing all our research, we came to what would be the hardest part of the process: writing our proposal for the Ben & Jerry's contest. It was very strenuous to take that amount of information and squeeze it eloquently into seven pages, the limit for the proposal. We made it through, however, and came out having learned the process of writing a grant proposal. Learning this skill is invaluable, because if you want to work on any kind of program bringing about social change, chances are that you will need to apply for a grant.

SHE WINS THE CONTEST!

Even with all the work we put into our proposal, we were still surprised and excited when we won the Ben & Jerry's contest. We immediately made the commitment to bring our plan into actuality by the end of the following school year. Unfortunately, Rachel had to move, and she was not able to return to Vermont Academy. That left the project in my hands.

FUND-RAISING AND "FRIEND-RAISING"

Rachel and I had accomplished a lot, but there was still so much more to do. I needed to start raising the money necessary to make my plan a reality. We first hired a wind consultant—a wind turbine engineer who helps people identify the correct placement for turbines and who is ultimately responsible for installing them. With the help of the consultant and my teacher, I was able to test the wind levels and find an appropriate place to put the turbine. Then we applied for grants and made phone calls asking people in our community for money. As part of our plan, Rachel and I had decided that we were going to raise all the money ourselves and not ask the school for a cent.

In addition to applying for grants and cold-calling people, I initiated a tree-sale fundraiser. Through flyers, newsletters, and e-mails, I advertised the sale to local residents, students, and the parents and families of our boarding students. All trees were sold on the basis of CO_2 reduction. I offered two different types of trees: quaking aspens and sugar maples. These grow at different rates and take carbon away from the atmosphere in a complementary way. Each tree absorbs a ton of carbon in its lifetime, believe it or

not! And the fund-raiser was a success. I was able to raise the balance of funds needed to cover the $53,000 project budget, as well as educate the local community about environmental issues.

IT ALL CAME TOGETHER

Throughout this process, I spent a lot of time speaking at school assemblies and town meetings and getting the word out through pamphlets and posters. I was determined to make this wind turbine an educational resource that everyone—students and adults alike—would be able to access. I planned for a link on our school Web site that people could visit to learn about how the project came about, how much energy was being produced, and details about alternative energy in general.

Finally, after months of hard work, the funds were secured, and the groundwork began two days before I graduated from high school. Nothing has ever made me so happy as knowing that this testament to all my hard work, as well as the hard work of all the others involved in the process, would soon stand forever on the campus of Vermont Academy.

WHAT'S NEXT FOR SAVANNAH?

When I look back, I realize that the hardest part was believing in myself, despite a lot of opposition and challenges. I think many people thought I'd give up and never finish a project this ambitious. It's scary to face a roomful of successful adults who assume you are just some dreamy teen, and try to convince them to put their faith and their money in your ability to help the world. But if you believe in the cause, you'll persevere.

Global warming, the death of biodiversity, waste, overuse of resources—all these things are unavoidably connected. Once I began educating myself and becoming active in trying to prevent, or lessen the effects of, global warming, I couldn't avoid becoming passionate about the rest of the Earth's problems as well.

I truly believe that wind is the energy of the future. It is the responsibility of our generation to seek energy alternatives that will ensure the sustainability of this planet and our culture, and fulfill the responsibilities we have to future generations. I know that the wind turbine at Vermont Academy is already serving a greater purpose by educating all who hear of or see it about the possibilities of green energy and the capabilities of students. Ultimately, the growing number of kids who are inspired by it is what matters most to me.

Savannah's TIP

Visit www.epa.gov and learn all you can about alternative energy. Ask your parents to contact your local power companies and elect to get all your electricity from alternative sources.

www.epa.gov

Lisa Sholk

Integrated Marketing Specialist for Ben & Jerry's Homemade, Inc.

Ben & Jerry's Lisa Sholk served scoopfuls of advice and guidance as Savannah's mentor on the contest she won.

Lisa Sholk develops promotions and campaigns for Ben & Jerry's based on the company's social mission. Not only does she get to be around ice cream all day, she communicates socially conscious initiatives she is so proud to be a part of as her business gives back to the community. From the Imagine Whirled Peace Campaign, to sustainable and safe methods of food production, to Licking Global Warming, Lisa believes in what her company stands for—leading with progressive values on a day-to-day basis.

Lisa's Tip: Take Action

The average American causes forty thousand pounds of harmful CO_2 emissions to be released into the Earth's atmosphere each year. There are simple actions we can all take to help curb global warming. Replace incandescent lightbulbs with fluorescent bulbs, do a couple loads of laundry in cold (or warm) water, carpool to work or other destinations, and recycle rather than throw everything in the trash.

Visit www.lickglobalwarming.org to find out just how much CO_2 you can save from the Earth's atmosphere. It's pretty remarkable what just one person can do.

www.lickglobalwarming.org

Making Dirt Clean and Toxin-Free

Emily Dellwig

Age: 18
Hometown:
Kansas City, Missouri

MEET EMILY AND HER CAUSE

I'm Emily Dellwig. I'm eighteen, and I'm from Kansas City. I love hanging out with friends, shopping for clothes, and playing all kinds of music—from jazz to heavy metal—on my electric bass guitar. But it's an entirely different type of heavy metals that makes me a green girl. I'm talking metal, as in elements that make up the periodic table, like copper, zinc, mercury, and lead. These metals are used in glass manufacturing, agriculture, and automobile manufacturing, and in the mining, electronics, and chemical industries. Lead contamination, in particular, is a huge problem in many parts of the world. From mining operations to industrial waste, lead can leach into the groundwater and soil, poisoning our food supply. Lead poisoning from paint, gasoline, or contaminated water or food can cause brain and nervous system damage, impair mental development in children, and harm reproductive systems, circulatory systems, and organs, like the kidneys.

Being a girl never stopped me from enrolling in as many science courses as I could. I enjoy learning and studying the sciences, and environmental issues were just something that interested me. I wanted to learn more about how I could help. When I realized that lead was a large problem in soil contamination, I knew I had to find out more.

EMILY'S EXPERIMENT GETS DOWN AND DIRTY

Although I have always been interested in the sciences, I had never done anything beyond the classroom. During my senior year in high school, I took a class in which each student conducted an independent experiment. I'd been thinking a lot about the current environmental crisis and wanted to do something to help. So I started with the basics—dirt. I wanted to find out what I could do to help clean up the soil. While researching soil contamination, I became interested in the effects of metal pollution, and I knew I had my topic for my solo experiment.

A MAGNETIC MOVE FOR THE PLANET

Working on this project, I discovered a simple way to take harmful chemicals, like lead, out of the ground. All it takes are some oranges and a battery—simple!

Oranges contain citric acid, which helps lead ions travel through the soil. Then the ions are adsorbed onto a gel made of liquefied orange peels, pulp, and juice mixed with calcium hydroxide. Adsorption means they stick onto the gel by forming a film rather than being absorbed into the gel.

Since conventional lead extraction and cleanup is extremely expensive, this process makes a lot of sense. It is organically based, requires very little equipment, and would provide cash-strapped orange farmers and juice manufacturers with an extra revenue source for fruits unsuitable for selling and for the remains of good fruit once the juice has been extracted. So it is doubly effective because it's a way to recycle oranges and other citrus produce that isn't a good enough quality to be sold as food.

The national attention my project received was completely unexpected. I think part of the attention came from the fact that scientists much older than myself had not really thought of this idea before.

TURNING THEORY INTO EVIDENCE

While my discovery was exciting, there were a few bumps in the road that I had to overcome. Finding literature that was related to my topic was one of the first problems that I encountered. I did a lot of my research at the library, which was a great source for scientific journals related to the topic I was studying. But even though I was able to find literature, my topic was not exactly a common one. The most useful resource was my teacher. The research and experiment was something that I did on my own, but she helped me a lot with planning my experiment and making sure that I was on track.

I faced a few other challenges once I began experimenting. Because this was my first experiment, I was unsure of where to start and how to carry it out. I had trouble setting up apparatuses that would make it possible for me to actually test the amount of lead in the soil. I also had a difficult time trying to perform lead tests because the orange juice would affect the color of the solution being tested. There were lots of smaller problems that I had to deal with, but that is just part of the process of scientific discovery. You have to persevere when frustrated by small setbacks and have the patience to work out the details, however long it takes.

EMILY'S IDEA GOES GLOBAL

Carrying out an experiment and finishing what I started is a huge accomplishment in itself. The fact that I won a few awards for my efforts was the icing on the cake. The most significant award was the Grand Award at the Greater Kansas City Science and Engineering

Fair, which included a trip to compete at the International Science and Engineering Fair (ISEF) in Atlanta, Georgia.

Attending the International Science and Engineering Fair was an amazing experience. There were competitors from all over the world. And there were opportunities to talk to Nobel laureates such as Dr. Rich Roberts, who won the Nobel Prize in Physiology or Medicine in 1993 for his discoveries in DNA. It was a great learning experience and very inspiring to know that young scientists can actually make a difference. I was interviewed by journalists interested in green technology, and Hank Green, an expert on the subject, blogged about me on his site www.ecogeek.org. I was grateful to have my work promoted and appreciated, that it would serve as an example to inspire other young scientists to follow through on their ideas.

Although I did not win any awards at ISEF, just being able to compete was enough for me to believe that what I did was important. Winning awards is great, but not everyone who tries to help the environment will receive public recognition, so you just have to look at what you have done to help the world. It's important to feel personal pride in your work, because what you do does make a difference.

A YOUNG SCIENTIST'S PROMISING FUTURE

Even though scientists have achieved so much, there is still a lot that needs to be done to clean up the environment. I may have worked with cleaning up the soil, but my research is just a small part of cleaning up soil pollution. And there is still so much that needs to be learned and discovered. There will always be problems that need to be fixed, and nothing will ever be perfect, but I know that we can come pretty close if people take the initiative, get involved, and try to make the world a better place.

I also want other girls to know that they can become scientists. Being educated about what the problems are is the first step to helping the environment. When I began my research, I was completely unaware of the extent of heavy metal pollution. Once we know what the problem is, we can take action to try to find a solution.

Emily's TIP

Even though I really enjoyed working on my experiment and competing in science fairs, the process was not always easy. I had to learn to maintain a balance between my work and the rest of my life. Being devoted to your work is great, but everyone deserves to have fun outside of the lab. Be proud of your accomplishments, even if nobody notices them. Finally, never let anyone tell you that you cannot do something. If something interests you, go after it, because you can do anything you set your mind to.

Sumi Cate

Sumi Cate is a group manager in research and development for the Green Works brand, a division of the Clorox family that develops cleaning products made with natural, plant-based ingredients. Sumi knows her way around a chemistry lab, and she's utilizing her science background to make the world of cleaning a greener place!

Sumi's Tip:
Consider a Career as a "Green-Collar" Worker

As our country ramps up its efforts to shift to a greener, cleaner economy, millions of "green-collar" jobs are forecast to be created over the next several years. My tip is to consider a career in green science and technology and take advantage of the exciting opportunities these jobs have to offer! More and more universities around the country are beginning to offer degree programs in "green" fields as they recognize the increasing demand for these types of workers. Now you can make a career out of being a green girl!

For more information, visit www.greenworks cleaners.com

Fuel Conservationist

Savannah *Walters*

Age: 16
Hometown:
Odessa, Florida

MEET SAVANNAH AND HER CAUSE

I'm Savannah Walters. I'm sixteen years old, and I live in Odessa, Florida, a state blessed with 1.5 million acres of natural wilderness—the Everglades. Some people think the Florida Everglades is just a barren swamp, but it is in fact the largest subtropical wilderness area in the United States, rich with wildlife and boasting many rare and endangered species. I've visited the area with my family many times, and I've learned to love its raw landscape. I learned at an early age the importance of keeping our wild areas wild, especially those in the farthest reaches of our planet.

When I was in second grade, our class did an eight-week study of the Arctic. And like the Everglades, some people think this region is nothing but a frozen, barren wasteland. But nothing could be further from the truth. The Arctic Coastal Plain is home to all sorts of animals, including gray wolves, grizzly bears, caribou, and hundreds of species of birds. The Arctic National Wildlife Refuge was established to protect and preserve these animals, but underneath this wild expanse of land are vast amounts of oil and natural gas reserves. Many people want to drill for oil in this wilderness. My teacher explained that politicians have

been trying for years to get approval to drill for oil in the refuge, which would effectively destroy it forever. How could we let this happen? I felt there had to be other options.

Then I met Lenny Comb, a wilderness photographer and environmental activist who shared my fascination for all things Arctic. He confirmed that there were other options to drilling, and that it came down to a very simple action that anyone could take. The fact is that Americans waste more than four million gallons of gas per day by driving on underinflated tires. We waste more gas than we would actually get out of the oils from the Arctic National Wildlife Refuge! I thought to myself, *Why don't people just pump up their tires?* It's hard for me to believe that eight years later I am still asking that question.

SAVANNAH CREATES PUMP 'EM UP

There are still many people who don't know they are wasting gas, polluting our air, and adding to global warming because they are driving on underinflated tires. I knew I had to do something. So with the help of my family and friends, I founded Pump 'Em Up. Our organization is a fuel conservation call to kids across the United States. We're spreading the word to drivers that the power to conserve fuel nationwide is in our own tires. The people who want to drill in the refuge talk about fancy tools and technologies they can use to get a little oil ten years from now. I have a tool that costs about ninety-nine cents that can save us four million gallons of gas a day—a tire gauge. But a big part of the problem is people don't know how to properly inflate their tires or how to use a tire gauge, and many times it's just not always convenient to pump up your tires.

At Pump 'Em Up, we give away free tire gauges and show people how to use them. You can go to our Web site at www.pumpemup.org to learn how to check gas mileage and how to properly inflate tires. It's really easy to see how much gas you can save if you check the mileage before and after your tires are properly inflated.

To get the word out, I did speaking engagements at schools. At one school, a student told me he got an electric scooter for Christmas and he charged the battery all night. The next day he rode the scooter for only an hour before the battery went dead. That night he charged the battery again, only this time he put more air in his tires. The next day, his battery lasted three hours! Pumping up your tires really makes a difference!

SAVANNAH STARTS FREE AIR STATIONS

One government study suggested that the main reason for people driving on underinflated tires is that people couldn't find reliable compressors to inflate their tires. A few months ago, my mom and I needed to fill a leaky tire; we had to go to four service stations before we could find one, and then it didn't work. So how could I make it easier and more convenient for people to pump up their tires? Since it was hard to find pumping stations, I decided to try to build free air stations. The first free air station was the idea of Phil Sumner in Albany, Georgia. He heard about Pump 'Em Up on the news and e-mailed me to ask if we would help him create a free air station for the 350 employees of his factory. They used an air compressor they already had and ran a hose out to a parking space. They painted it green and put a Pump 'Em Up banner up so they can all do their part to reduce air pollution and save gas.

That was just the beginning. The second Pump 'Em Up free air station is at the University of North Carolina (UNC) at Charlotte. They put in a whole station with a new compressor for all the students, faculty, and anyone else in the community to use. We are challenging all the universities in the United States to follow UNC's example and put a Pump 'Em Up station on their campus. I have set up stations monthly in my community where we pump up tires for free and hand out tire gauges.

CHALLENGES DIDN'T STOP SAVANNAH!

The greatest struggle for me has been to get my own state representatives in Congress to cast their votes to protect the environment. I have given speeches, written letters, signed petitions, and attended rallies, all in an effort to encourage politicians to vote to protect the Arctic. I spent five days in Washington, D.C., as a guest of the Alaska Wilderness League, lobbying my Florida legislators about the need to conserve fuel to clean up our air and preserve the Arctic National Wildlife Refuge. I joined Senator Maria Cantwell, Senator John Kerry, and Senator Joe Lieberman in a Senate rally. I spoke about my organization in the Capitol alongside these senators. I was doubly honored when, in April 2008, I was awarded the inaugural Captain Planet Young

Eco Award for my environmental activism and for encouraging innovative projects that empower today's children as environmental stewards. While it was thrilling to have my efforts recognized, the press coverage of the event helped bring even more attention to the need to conserve fuel as a means to preserve the Arctic wilderness.

WHAT'S NEXT FOR SAVANNAH?

My goal for Pump 'Em Up is to help new drivers create good habits by checking their tire pressure at least once a month. I also want to help experienced drivers understand how important it is to check their tire pressure regularly. After more than eight years of active campaigning, we still have a long way to go to get everyone to understand the connection between tire pressure, fuel consumption, and keeping our wilderness pristine. It is our job to keep our world clean. So before we start drilling and destroy the last vestiges of wilderness on our planet, the least we can do is . . . Pump 'Em Up!

 # Savannah's TIP

Be sure to have your parents check their tire pressure every month, especially before making a long trip or pulling a heavy load. Here's how:

• Always use the inflation recommended by the vehicle manufacturer. You can find this information in the car owner's manual, on the inside of the glove box door, or posted on the edge of the driver's-side door.

• Use a reliable gauge. *This is very important!*

• To get a true tire pressure reading, check the tires when they're cold and when the vehicle has been idle for at least three hours.

Shannon Babb

GOING BUGGY FOR WATER QUALITY

The 4-H pledge:
As a true 4-H member
I pledge my head to clearer thinking,
my heart to greater loyalty,
my hands to larger service,
and my health to better living,
for my club, my community,
my country, and my world.

Many green girls, like Shannon Babb, start out early on their eco adventures as 4-H members. The four *Hs* stand for Head, Heart, Hands, and Health. 4-H has more than 6.5 million members, ages five to nineteen, across America who are learning and working in programs about citizenship, healthy living, and science, engineering, and technology.

Meet Shannon Babb and Her Cause

I'm Shannon Babb, I'm twenty, and I attend Utah State University where I am majoring in watershed earth systems. My interest in the quality of water stems from my time spent in 4-H. I started in 4-H as a third-grader in the cookie club. I slowly branched out to try acting and art, but discovered I loved science and joined more science-based clubs. A few years later, I enrolled in a class on water quality and was hooked after the hands-on experience. I collected water and insect samples from the American Fork River, conducted chemical analyses, and discussed what the results meant. My dad and I even formed a new 4-H water-quality club.

Water, Water Everywhere

Today, I'm still a loyal collegiate member of 4-H. I completed two research projects through my college club. The first, "The Ins and Outs of Utah Lake," was a six-month study of the chemicals and plastic traces in the waters of the lake's tributaries. The second, "Going Buggy," tested the same waters, this time for the biological aspects of bugs. Looking at that indicates how healthy the ecosystem is. I am now trying to educate people on how to keep their local water sources cleaner.

I am passionate about clean water and sometimes teach a class at my county 4-H. Water quality is one of the biggest issues facing the world today. Diseases caused by contaminated water is the number one cause of death for kids under five. To combat this, I not only study polluted water but clean water as well. We need to find a solution to this growing crisis, and I intend to be part of this solution.

Shannon's Tip

Hands-on experiences are critical to get people interested in science. Our academic system is moving more toward tests, which cuts out time for the hands-on exploration of our world. It's getting harder to find organizations that really allow you to explore. And you don't have to be a genius to be great at science . . . you just have to love it.

Learn more about how you can join the 4-H and get hands-on experience in a field you love. Go to www.4-h.org.

www.4-h.org

Colette Brooks

Chief Imagination Officer of Big Imagination Group (BIG)

How I learned to Kick Gas

I wasn't born an eco-activist. I found it over time, or rather it found me. Despite growing up in a female-dominated household, I had a peculiar penchant for big muscle cars. Little did I know that these gas guzzlers were horrible for the environment.

Going Green

So when did I do a one-eighty? It started with a horse and my discovery of nature as I rode through the unspoiled trails of the Santa Monica Mountains. Add to that my introduction to some green practices, like composting and the benefits of using

reusable commuter mugs, grocery bags, and cloth hand towels instead of paper. Those waste-reduction practices led me to connect the dots between the lifestyle choices I made and the impact those choices had on the survival of the planet. Instantly, I became a grown-up green girl!

On a roll

As my interest in sustainability grew, so did my quest to reduce my carbon footprint. In 2002, I discovered the gas-sipping, clean-burning Prius hybrid and bought a small fleet for my advertising agency, around which I generated significant press as the first private company in the United States to acquire a hybrid fleet. I was so smitten with the technology that in 2003, I convinced a handful of celebrities to take chauffeur-driven Priuses instead of gas-guzzling limos to the Academy Awards. And that's when everything changed. The nerdy little Prius was on the road to becoming the Hollywood "it" car the moment Leo DiCaprio, Cameron Diaz, and Harrison Ford stepped out of it and onto the red carpet. The green movement got its first taste of Hollywood gold.

Kick Gas

Making the leap from my gas-sipping Prius to kicking the petrol habit altogether came quite naturally. In 2004, I was introduced to biodiesel, a vegetable-based renewable fuel source that eliminates the need for oil drilling, emits 78 percent fewer CO_2 emissions than gasoline, and is grown and processed right here in the United States. The only thing I needed was a car with a diesel engine. So I found a 1979 Cadillac El Dorado diesel that not only satisfied my love of muscle cars, but allowed me to indulge in an eco-friendly way. And that was the inspiration for Biobling (www.biobling.com).

Originally founded to help spread the word, Biobling quickly became an online resource that connects conscious consumers to bioready cars and the renewable fuel to run them. It was a pretty simple concept, really. The biocurious would visit the Biobling site, submit a simple form with their driving requirements and budget, and we'd scour the city, state, country, and find clients the biorides of their dreams . . . or budgets as the case may be. The trickier part was gaining convenient access to the fuel. So a group of my biobuddies and I formed the L.A. Biodiesel Co-op, which turned out to be a series of trailers situated around Los Angeles that serve as mobile filling stations for co-op members. The concept was so successful, it demonstrated significant market demand and was the catalyst that convinced three brick-and-mortar gas stations to offer biodiesel at the pump.

Tips to help your parents to kick gas

1) Ride your bike or take the bus—public transportation is super efficient and environmentally responsible.

2) If you need to use a car, sell your gas vehicle and replace it with a good, used diesel car. Diesel engines can go for 200,000 to 300,000 miles before they need to be overhauled. So for a fraction of the cost of a new car, you can reduce waste by giving a used diesel vehicle a second life (sparing the already overflowing landfill) and protect the environment by running it on a clean, renewable fuel source.

3) If you're looking for convenience, you can fill up with biodiesel from the pump or from your local co-op. For the more adventurous and thrifty eco-warriors, you can convert your diesel engine to run on waste vegetable oil (WVO), which you can collect yourself from local restaurants.

My Green Girl Pledge

Now that you have read the stories of the wonderful things these green girls are accomplishing all over the country, we hope that you will be inspired to bring more green into your own life. Share this book with your friends, classmates, or a school or local library. Think about all the different environmental tips our Green Girls have contributed and pick one (or more!) that makes the most sense to you as a personal green starting point.

THERE ARE LOTS OF THINGS YOU CAN DO!

Opt for safe, toxin-free beauty, bath, and body care like Erin.

Create the perfect reusable bag like Adrienne.

Reinvent your wardrobe like Maya.

Reduce waste by recycling party dresses like Caitlin.

Help protect the animals you love like Stephanie.

Clean up a local waterway or beach like Chelsea and Elizabeth.

Champion an endangered species like Mollie.

Investigate green pet-care options like Honor.

Campaign to save the rain forest like Rebecca.

Share your green thoughts through poetry like Simone.

Cheer for the planet like Devyn.

Get crafty and quilt your green message like Casey.

Reduce your carbon footprint like Isabel.

Rethink your use of plastics like Zoe.

Be a good green tourist like Sibella.

Set up community recycling systems like Janee, Linda, and Vanessa.

Throw a green party like Jordan H.

Freshen up your school menu with organic produce like Amelia.

Support family farms and farmers markets like Araceli.

Do green activities with the kids you babysit like Noa.

Stand up for your rights to clean air like Erica.

Take action to save land sacred to your community like Alberta.

Help make someone else's city green like Jordan S.

Generate awareness of water scarcity like Emily W.

Build a source of alternative power for your school like Savannah.

Research scientific methods to greening our planet like Emily D.

Conserve fuel like Savannah W.

Investigate solutions to water quality like Shannon.

OR START SMALL...

Take an environmental or earth science class.

Volunteer to help green your school.

Help your family green your home.

Find out more about green-collar careers.

Work with animals to preserve local habitats.

Work to protect endangered species.

Find out where your food comes from.

Help make sure the food you eat is safe and healthy.

Support legislation to enforce cosmetic manufacturers to ensure the safety of their products.

Investigate the recycling practices of your home, school, and community.

Work with local government to resolve environmental problems.

Raise funds for a cause you believe in.

Join one of the organizations in this book.

I, _____, have gone green. As a green girl I promise to think about how my personal behavior and habits affect the planet. Every little bit counts and I will do my part to be green from this day forward.

_____

NOTE FROM THE AUTHOR

I used to think I was a pretty green person—I recycled, supported green groups, bought organic, checked for fair-trade certification, didn't let the water run when I brushed my teeth, and always, always, always turned out lights. . . but I had never come across any carbon footprints, a term that kept coming up during meetings at my new job at Participant Media. In late 2005, I was hired to work on the early pre-theatrical release campaign for the film *An Inconvenient Truth.* Mystified, I went to the resident green expert on the team, Lisa Day (who is so green that even her shoes are made out of hemp!), and asked her where I could pick up a pair of these carbon footprints, which, in my mind, were some kind of super-eco odor-eating shoe insoles that absorbed heat and pollution. Thank God they didn't throw me out to the curb right then and there.

With great patience, Lisa explained to me the green basics and helped me calculate my carbon footprint. In doing so, I had a good overview of the impact (numerically) I was personally making on the planet. I changed some of my habits, got a hybrid car, adjusted the thermostat, took canvas bags to the market, and cut out plastic bottles, but being green was still a daunting jumble of facts and figures, and the idea of ME having the ability to curb global warming by my little behavioral changes was also still too abstract. It was too scary to think about the responsibility of saving the whole planet and much easier to feel all gloom and doom about the situation. I didn't feel confident that my individual actions really made any difference at all.

Ironically, one of my duties was to manage outreach to teachers and students to see the film and get them involved in our social action programs. It was at the first of these high school field trips to a special screening of the film that the calculations translated into real actions. Hundreds of students streamed out of the theater, totally psyched to take action. They bombarded me with questions and asked for resources and had so many great ideas and such enthusiasm. They wanted to DO SOMETHING, and, for the most part, do something is exactly what they did. These passionate young environmentalists became my teachers. And they didn't wait for adults to tell them what to do or how to do it. They were not scared or intimidated by the task of saving the planet. There was work to do, all kinds of ways to help, and every little bit of effort was needed and appreciated.

Over the last four years, I have had the honor and pleasure of meeting so many young people working on a vast spectrum of environmental initiatives, and a majority of these young green activists are girls. Perhaps it is natural for girls, who may one day be mothers, as well as working professionals, to feel especially nurturing. Some of the young women profiled in this handbook have earned national recognition for their achievements, while others are making strides on more local levels. Some are packing up for college, while others are still packing their lunches for elementary school. Each and every one of the girls profiled in this book is an eco hero who offers hope and direction for her generation.

I would like to thank all the green girls and experts who shared their stories within these pages, with a special thank-you to Hayden Panettiere for her inspiring foreword, and also the following people for their contributions toward the creation of this book.

Story Editors: I am grateful to Jenny Mancino and Diana Mendez, my main green girl guides throughout this process, without whose help this book would not be possible. Thank you for your diligent research, creative support, and most of all, patience!

Editorial Assistants: Ariana Gadd, Chris Eggertsen, Sarah Newman, EK Peyton, Ashley Doyle, and Rachel Stratman for all their hard work keeping facts, details, and ME on track. You guys are amazing!

Interns: Camilla Savoia, Jake Gissy, Lindsay Weller, Paulina Bolinski, and Glenna Moran for their unbridled enthusiasm. Awesome!

Green Publishing Pros: Merrilee Heifetz of Writers House; Penguin's Eileen Kreit, Doug Whiteman, Karen Chaplin, Kristin Gilson, and Alaina Wong; and Nancy Cushing-Jones, Barbara Weller, and Cynthia Cleveland of Broadthink. Thank you for giving me this opportunity.

Special thanks to my colleagues at Participant Media, with a great big green shout-out to Ricky Strauss for being the first in line to support my idea for this book years before I really knew what it was about. To my two amazing mentors, Buffy Shutt and Kathy Jones, who always seem to know what's best for me and who constantly surprise me by never saying no to my harebrained schemes. Thank you to Jeff Skoll for now having inspired me to write THREE books. His mission to create socially conscious media that inspires and compels social change is something I try to emulate. I'm grateful to Jim Berk, our head honcho, for his leadership and his vision. Thanks also to Jeff Ivers, Bob Murphy, and Gabriel Brakin for their investment in and continued support for my adventures in publishing. A great big hug to my dear marketing partners-in-crime Karen "Ariel The Mermaid" Frankel, Amanda "Gossip Girl" Garrison, Jeff "Brussels Griffon 3X" Sakson, and Youtchi "Dior" von Lintel. A tip of the hat to our social action team for the good work they do every day: Bonnie Abaunza, Christina Lindstrom, John Schreiber, Liana Schwarz, and Daniel Maree. A salute to our "AIT" mavens: Diane Weyerman, Courtney Sexton, Bryan Stamp, and Yelena Rachitsky. A nod to our digital wizards: Fonda Berosini, Wendy Cohen, Joshua Tremblay, and Chris Gebhardt. A green wave to Analiza Gonzales, Laurie Luh, and Mai Imai for always keeping an eye out for me.

Connectors: Jeff Pantukhoff, Claire Jones, Kelly Bush, Tara Walls, Danica Krislovich, Susan Paley, Alice Markowitz, Carmelle Druchniak, Aileen Zerrudo, Iris Yen, Delphia Duckens, Thameenah Muhammad, Michelle Tompkins, Sandey Kang, Michelle Kydd Lee, Maureen Harrington, Jane Berk, Amy Chendar, Brian Gerber, Michelle Kleinert Bader, Michael Donkis, Sue Patricola, Randy Smith, Michelle Ferguson, Jennifer DeVito, Andrew Barker, Lori Tabb, Jill Calcaterra, Robert Jigarjian, Jennifer Bubalo Sloan, Archie Drury, Tom Rielly, Gary Hirshberg, Jack Merrill, Nathalie Harewood, Livia Firth, Pat and Nigel Sinclair, Sharon Lawrence, and my fellow WIFF Trustees.

Family and Friends: Pola Hirshfield, Burton Hirshfield, Suzanne Hirshfield, and Eli Pearl; Susan Cartsonis, Andy Cohen, Ian Corson, Jay Corson, Laura Edwards, Margi English, Nana Greenwald, Aline Grunwald, Jesse and Stephen Nathan, Jackie Papier, Barbara Perlin, and Gina and Chris Shelton.

My green tip to readers: Please consider spaying or neutering your pets! Help control pet overpopulation and please consider adopting your next dog from a shelter. I support K-9 Connection, an organization that brings the magic of dogs and kids together. At-risk teens ages fourteen to eighteen train homeless shelter dogs in basic obedience, assisting the dogs to develop the skills to become adoptable. For more information, please visit www.k9connection.org.

PHOTO CREDITS

RESOURCES FOR GREEN GIRLS

WEB SITES

4-H	www.4-h.org
Alaska Youth for Environmental Action	www.ayea.org
Alliance for Climate Education	www.acespace.org
American Community Gardening Association	www.communitygarden.org
Arbor Day Foundation	www.arborday.org
Association of Zoos and Aquariums	www.aza.org
Ben & Jerry's	www.benjerry.com
Bergey Wind Power	www.bergey.com
Best Friends Animal Society	www.bestfriends.org
Blanket the Globe	www.blankettheglobe.com
British Council	www.britishcouncil.com
Brower Youth Awards	www.broweryouthawards.org
Caitlin's Closet	www.caitlinscloset.org
California Air Resources Board	www.arb.ca.gov
California Climate Champions	www.climatechamps.org
California State Lands Commission	www.slc.ca.gov
Central Coast Alliance United for a Sustainable Economy	www.coastalalliance.com
Clean Air Council	www.cleanair.org
Climate Crisis	www.climatecrisis.net/takeaction/carboncalculator/
The Climate Project	www.theclimateproject.org
Clorox Greenworks	www.cloroxgreenworks.com
CNN	www.cnn.com
The Daily Green	www.thedailygreen.com
Disney Family	www.disneyfamily.com
Disney Friends for Change	www.disney.go.com/projectgreen
Donors Choose	www.donorschoose.org
Earth 911	www.earth911.org

Earthbox	www.earthbox.com
Earth Echo International	www.earthecho.org
Eat Well Guide	www.eatwellguide.org
Eco Age	www.eco-age.com
Ecogeek	www.ecogeek.com
The Ecological Footprint quiz	www.myfootprint.org
Ecorazzi	www.ecorazzi.com
Emma Willard School	www.emmawillard.org
Endangered Species Coalition	www.stopextinction.org
Environmental Media Association	www.ema-online.org
Firestone Tires	www.firestonecompleteautocare.com
Florida Fish and Wildlife Conservation Commission	www.myfwc.com
Food & Water Watch	www.foodandwaterwatch.org
Girl Scouts of America	www.girlscouts.org
Girls' Life	www.girlslife.com
Global Green USA	www.globalgreen.org
Good Year Tires	www.goodyear.com
Green Ambassadors	www.greenambassadors.org
Green Cross International	www.gci.ch
Green Gear Bags	www.greengearbag.com
Green Mountain Power	www.greenmountainpower.com
Grist	www.grist.org
Habitat for Humanity International	www.habitat.org
Hubbs-SeaWorld Research Institute	www.hswri.org
Intel Science Talent Search	www.intel.com/education/sts/
International Exotic Animal Sanctuary	www.bigcat.org
The Jane Goodall Institute	www.janegoodall.org
K9 Connection	www.k9connection.org
Kids Making a Difference	www.kmad.org
Lick Global Warming	www.lickglobalwarming.org

Local Harvest	www.localharvest.org
Me to We	www.metowe.org
Michelin Group	www.michelin.com
National Wildlife Federation	www.nwf.org
The Nature Conservancy	www.nature.org/initiatives/climatechange/calculator/
Newspaper Association of America	www.naa.org
O_2 for Life	www.o2forlife.org
Openlands	www.openlands.org
Outward Bound	www.outwardbound.com
Pacific Whale Foundation	www.pacificwhale.org
Peta Kids	www.petakids.com
Pinellas County Government	www.pinellascounty.org
Plenticulture	www.plenticulture.com
Pump 'Em Up	www.pumpemup.org
Rainforest Action Network	www.ran.org
Rocking the Boat	www.rockingtheboat.org
Roots & Shoots	www.rootsandshoots.org
Roxy	www.roxy.com
Save the Arctic Blog	www.savethearctic.blogspot.com
Save the Children	www.savethechildren.org
Save the Peaks Coalition	www.savethepeaks.org
Save the Whales Again!	www.savethewhalesagain.com
Seeds of Change	www.seedsofchange.com
Solar Now	www.solarnow.com
South Central Farmers	www.southcentralfarmers.com
Stonyfield Farms	www.stonyfield.com
Sustainable Table	www.sustainabletable.org
The Tap Project	www.tapproject.org
Teens Turning Green	www.teensturninggreen.org
Treehugger	www.treehugger.com

TreePeople	www.treepeople.org
UNICEF	www.unicef.org
Urban Harvest	www.urbanharvest.org
U.S. Department of Energy	www.energy.gov
U.S. Department of Transportation	www.dot.gov/new/index.htm
U.S. Environmental Protection Agency	www.epa.gov
U.S. Fish and Wildlife Service	www.fws.gov
Vermont Academy	www.vermontacademy.org
Vermont Renewable Energy Resource Center	www.rerc-vt.org
Water.org	www.water.org
The Whaleman Foundation	www.whaleman.org
Whole Foods Market	www.wholefoodsmarket.com
The Women's Conference	www.womensconference.org
Worldwatch Institute	www.worldwatch.org
World Wildlife Fund	www.worldwildlife.org
Youth Speaks	www.youthspeaks.org
Zero Footprint Kids	www.zerofootprintkids.com

BOOKS AND ARTICLES

Brown, Lester R. *Plan B 2.0: Rescuing a Planet Under Stress and a Civilization in Trouble.* W. W. Norton & Company, 2003.

Caldeira, Ken. "When Being Green Raises the Heat." *New York Times*, January 16, 2007.

Diaz, E., ed. *Microbial Biodegradation: Genomics and Molecular Biology.* Caister Academic Press, 2008.

Lovins, Amory B. "More Profit with Less Carbon." *Scientific American*, September 2005.

Pirog, Rich, and Andrew Benjamin. *Checking the Food Odometer: Comparing Food Miles for Local Versus Conventional Produce Sales in Iowa Institutions."* Leopold Center for Sustainable Agriculture, July 2003.

Taylor, Leslie. *The Healing Power of Rainforest Herbs.* Square One Publishers, 2005.